# The Shipment

"Cultural images of black Americ̲    ̲.̲,̲c̲a̲K̲e̲d̲, pulled and twisted like Silly Putty in *The Shipment*, a subversive, seriously funny new theater piece by the adventurous playwright Young Jean Lee . . . Combing through the images of African Americans that dominate the media, Ms. Lee wields sharp, offbeat humor to point up the clichés, distortions and absurdities . . . Ms. Lee sets you thinking about how we unconsciously process experience—at the theater, or in life—through the filter of racial perspective, and how hard it can be to see the world truly in something other than black and white."

—Charles Isherwood, *New York Times*

"Lee is a facetious provocateur; that is, she does whatever she can to get under our skin—with laughs and with raw, brutal talk . . . Lee makes her audience walk a knife's edge of race and meaning. How does blackness sound? And how have we been conditioned to hear black speech? . . . This is so ingenious a twist, such a radical bit of theatrical smoke and mirrors, that, in rethinking everything that has come before . . . we are forced to confront our own preconceived notions of race. And to agree with Lee that we may not live long enough to purge ourselves of them."

—Hilton Als, *New Yorker*

"In this discomforting but viciously goofy mélange, Lee confirms herself as one of the best experimental playwrights in America. Her language manages to be both feverishly strange and rigorously intellectual . . . Ethnic jokes abound here; some might be on you."

—David Cote, *TimeOut New York*

# LEAR

"In *LEAR*, Young Jean Lee's self-described 'inaccurate distortion' of the classic, she banishes the title monarch and Gloucester to the wings and focuses on the younger generation . . . The absurdist, meta-Shakespearean results are by turns irreverent, grotesque and morally harrowing . . . Lee is one of the most vital, rewarding playwrights to arrive on the scene in the past decade. *LEAR* has power and ought to endure."

—David Cote, *TimeOut New York*

"Lee uses *King Lear* and some beautifully unconventional additions to flesh out Shakespeare's themes of loneliness, mortality and filial responsibility in gratifying and moving depth."

—Sam Thielman, *Variety*

"Young Jean's *LEAR* is Shakespeare's rotated in four-dimensional space to reveal what is lost in most productions (ghastly, sentimental parodies for the most part—Bard shibboleths): the cold, hard claims of nothingness—the implacable something/nothing out of which we all come, and into which we vanish without a trace. The simple power of the work is terrific, often sardonic, always relentless; *LEAR* is certainly Lee's best work yet."

—Mac Wellman

The Shipment

LEAR

# The Shipment
# LEAR

Young Jean Lee

Theatre Communications Group    New York    2010

This publication is made possible in part with public funds from the New York State Council on the Arts, a State Agency.

TCG books are exclusively distributed to the book trade by Consortium Book Sales and Distribution.

Library of Congress Cataloging-in-Publication Data
Lee, Young Jean.
The shipment and Lear / Young Jean Lee.—1st ed.
p. cm.
ISBN 978-1-55936-356-3
I. Title.
PS3612.E228S55    2010
812'.6—dc22    2010008790

Book design and composition by Lisa Govan
Cover design by Lisa Govan
Cover photos by Sara Krulwich/New York Times/Redux (front); Lisa Kereszi (back)

First Edition, June 2010

In memory of James M. Lee,
great thinker, non-complainer,
and loving father

# Contents

# The Shipment

For Mike Farry

Production History

*The Shipment* premiered in January 2009 at The Kitchen in New York City. It was co-commissioned by the Wexner Center for the Arts at The Ohio State University and The Kitchen, and produced by Young Jean Lee's Theater Company (Young Jean Lee, Artistic Director; Caleb Hammons, Producing Director). It was written and directed by Young Jean Lee. It was produced by Caleb Hammons. The set design was by David Evans Morris, the lighting design was by Mark Barton, the costume design was by Roxana Ramseur, the sound design was by Matthew Tierney and the choreography was by Faye Driscoll. It was performed by:

| | |
|---|---|
| DANCER 2, SIDEKICK MICHAEL, CRACKHEAD JOHN, BAD COP 2, SASHAY, OMAR | Mikéah Ernest Jennings |
| DANCER 1, DRUG DEALER DESMOND, RECORD COMPANY EXECUTIVE, SINGER 2, DESMOND | Prentice Onayemi |
| RAPPER OMAR, SINGER 3, MICHAEL | Okieriete Onodowan |
| STAND-UP COMEDIAN, GRANDPA JOE, PAUL THE EXTREME, BAD COP 1, THOMAS | Douglas Scott Streater |
| MAMA, DRUG DEALER MAMA, VIDEO HO, GRANDMA FROM HEAVEN, SINGER 1, THOMASINA | Amelia Workman |

| STAGEHAND 1 | Joseph John |
| STAGEHAND 2 | Foteos Macrides |

An earlier version of *The Shipment* premiered in 2008 at the Wexner Center for the Arts in Columbus, with the same production team. It was performed by:

| DANCER 2, SIDEKICK MICHAEL, CRACKHEAD JOHN, BAD COP 2, SASHAY, OMAR | Mikéah Ernest Jennings |
| DANCER 1, DRUG DEALER DESMOND, RECORD COMPANY EXECUTIVE, SINGER 2, DESMOND | Prentice Onayemi |
| RAPPER OMAR, SINGER 3, THOMAS | Jordan Barbour |
| STAND-UP COMEDIAN, GRANDPA JOE, PAUL THE EXTREME, BAD COP 1, MICHAEL | Douglas Scott Streater |
| MAMA, DRUG DEALER MAMA, VIDEO HO, DENISE, WENDY, GRANDMA FROM HEAVEN, SINGER 1, THOMASINA | Amelia Workman |
| STAGEHAND 1 | Edward Hawkins |
| STAGEHAND 2 | Joe McCutcheon |

Author's Note

The show is divided into two parts. The first half is structured like a minstrel show—dance, stand-up routine, sketches, and a song—and I wrote it to address the stereotypes my cast members felt they had to deal with as black performers. Our goal was to walk the line between stock forms of black entertainment and some unidentifiable weirdness to the point where the audience wasn't sure what they were watching or how they were supposed to respond. The performers wore stereotypes like ill-fitting paper-doll outfits held on by two tabs, which denied the audience easy responses (illicit pleasure or self-righteous indignation) to racial clichés and created a kind of uncomfortable, paranoid watchfulness in everyone. The second half of the show is a relatively straight naturalistic comedy. I asked the actors to come up with roles they'd always wanted to play and wrote the second half of the show in response to their requests.

*A bare stage. Stark lights. Ominous white noise in the background.*
*Sudden lights down.*
*Sound of footsteps.*
*Sound of shoes clattering against the floor as Dancer 1 begins his*
*dance in the dark.*
*A rock song—Semisonic's "F.N.T."—begins.*
*Lights up on Dancer 1 mid-jump, his arms and legs sprawling. He*
*is wearing a black tuxedo with a white shirt, black suspenders, black*
*cummerbund, and black bow tie.*

*Dancer 1 performs a series of bordering-on-goofy choreographed*
*moves that are unidentifiable in genre. Occasionally we'll see a flash of*
*possible minstrel reference—a gesture, a bit of footwork. Sometimes*
*Dancer 1 is smiling, sometimes not. It's difficult to tell what his rela-*
*tionship is to what he's doing and to the audience.*

*Dancer 2 enters and watches Dancer 1, looking bemused. He is*
*wearing a black suit, white shirt, flowered vest, red tie, black flower lapel*
*brooch, and white shoes.*

*He starts to shake violently, still smiling. The two Dancers take*
*turns doing herky-jerky movements and then flail wildly back and forth*
*across the stage, sometimes syncing up to flail in unison. It's reminiscent*
*of a tap routine, except that neither of them has any coordination and*
*they look as if they are about to fall.*

*They break out of the flailing and walk in a square pattern around the perimeter of the stage, stopping downstage to stare at the audience. Then they move upstage to do a partner dance that involves Dancer 2 shaking violently in place while Dancer 1 twirls around him, grabbing hold of Dancer 2's stiff, jerking hands as he dips and spins.*

*For the big finish, both Dancers take turns doing fancy spins with their arms out. Dancer 1 breaks the pattern to do a goofy little jump. Dancer 2 does an even goofier move. Dancer 1 runs up to the back wall and touches it with his butt. Dancer 2 follows suit. Both Dancers push themselves off the back wall and collapse onto the floor downstage, standing up crookedly to do a little half-smiling hat-tip to the audience before walking offstage.*

"*F.N.T.*" *lyrics:*

Fascinating new thing
You delight me
And I know you're speaking of me

Fascinating new thing
Get beside me,
I want you to love me

I'm surprised that you've never been told before
That you're lovely and you're perfect
And that somebody wants you

Fascinating new thing
The scene makin'
Want a temporary savior

Fascinating new thing
Don't betray them
By becoming familiar

I'm surprised that you've never been told before
That you're lovely and you're perfect
And that somebody wants you

I'm surprised that you've never been told before
That you're priceless and you're precious
Even when you are not new.

I'm surprised that you've never been told before
That you're lovely and you're perfect
And that somebody wants you

I'm surprised that you've never been told before
That you're priceless
Yeah, you're holy
Even when you are not new

Fascinating new thing (fascinating new thing)
Fascinating new thing (fascinating new thing)
Fascinating new thing (fascinating new thing)
Fascinating new thing (fascinating new thing).

*(A rap song, Lil Jon's "I Don't Give a Fuck," begins as the dance ends.)*

ANNOUNCER *(Into offstage mike)*: *(Name of city!)*
Please put cho mothafuckin' hands together for the one, the only, *(Name of actor playing Stand-Up Comedian!)*

*(Stand-Up Comedian runs onstage to the music. He is wearing a black tux with a white shirt and skinny black tie.*

*He stops downstage left and mimes having sex doggy style while facing the audience. He mimes wiping his imaginary partner's crotch from the rear, smells his fingers, makes a disgusted face, and kicks her away as he goes into a "superman" dance move.*

*He runs downstage center, turns his back to the audience, looks coyly over his shoulder at them, starts jiggling his ass, and then drops his booty like a stripper.*

*He runs downstage right and does the "tootsie roll" dance, ending with his fist in the air as he spins around and grabs his mike from its stand offstage right.*

*The music stops.)*

STAND-UP COMEDIAN: *(Name of city!) (Name of city)* mothafuckin'
*(Name of state or country)* up in this! Wassup, bitches?! Where
*(Location appropriate reference such as "Brooklyn" or "My Bears
Fans" or "The Parisians")* at? *(He calls out the name of a rich neigh-
borhood in the city he's in)*

*(The cast backstage makes woofing noises à la* The Arsenio Hall
Show.*)*

See, that's my shit ya'll. I'm a *(Name of rich neighborhood in city)*
nigga born and bred—that's right! GOOD to be back in *(Name
of city)*. GOOD to be back. Got some good memories about this
place here. Some real shit.

Had these two little girlfriends when I was seven. One white
and one black. Never gave me the pussy though. Never. Used
to let me watch. They'd come over to my house and start rub-
bin' they pussies together, and one of 'em used to fuck herself
with a pencil! Yeah! Used to fuck herself with a number two
pencil until she came, or as she liked to call it, "Passed her
test." That bitch had straight A's when it came to that shit!

*(He gives the audience a "What's your problem?" look.)*

What! This mothafucka be lookin' at me like, *(He singles someone out in the audience and imitates a white guy voice)* "That man
is a pedophile!" I ain't no pedophile, nigga! YOU a fuckin'
pedophile for thinkin' 'bout it in a pedophiliac way!

Kids be some nasty-ass freaks, man! Oh, don't act like you
ain't neva seen a three year old humpin' a sofa cushion! *(He
humps the air and smacks an imaginary sofa cushion as if it's an
ass)* "You take that, sofa cushion! Take that, TAKE THAT."

Now if black mama see that shit? Maaan, you betta hope
that kid get to keep his dick! Black mama be like, *(He makes vio-
lent hitting noise and gesture)* "Mothafucka, you KNOW we rent-
ed this shit! Now put some ice on yo' eye and get dressed. We
gotta go to church and pray for yo' little demon ass!" And
that's how putting plastic on furniture got started.

Now, a white mama? White mama don't know how to deal
with this shit! White mama be like, "Chad? Do you know why

Daddy and I always smell like wet dog? It's because we fuck goats." And that's how syphilis got started.

Now, I know some a you thinkin', "Why do black comedians still do those, 'White people are like this, and black people are like that' jokes?"

Well, I'm a tell you why. Now I don't mean to be offensive by sayin' this, but——white people be evil.

*(He gives the audience a deadly serious look.)*

Naw, I'm just playin' witch'all. Most white folks ain't evil— they just stupid. White people be some a the stupidest mothafuckas on the planet. You think I ENJOY talkin' 'bout race? I wanna talk about POOP, mothafucka!

Shit, there ain't nothin' funnier to me than poop. When I'm at home that's practically all I wanna talk about. My wife, she can't take it. Finally it got to be too much for her and she started threatenin' to stop suckin' my dick, so I had to stop. But I still needed an outlet to express my feelins, so I came up with the poop FACE.

*(He makes the poop face.)*

Now, I'm not allowed to talk about poop in my wife's presence, but when I make the poop face, she KNOW what I'm thinkin' 'bout.

*(He makes the poop face.)*

But I can't talk about poop. Nope. I gotta talk about RACE because white people be some stupid-ass mothafuckas.

[To be added in applicable countries outside the United States:] And don't think I'm just talkin' 'bout Americans, neither. *(Imitating local accent)* "Ha ha ha, those stupid Americans. We do not have such race problems here in *(Name of country)*." So y'all don't got no race problems in *(Name of country)*? Mothafuckas, you KNOW your shit is fucked-up, too! *(Name of city)* got plenty a niggas—y'all just call 'em *(Name of ethnicity)*.

And y'all be like, "For us it is not about race, it is about nation-ality and religion." But the fact that y'all don't SOCIALIZE with YOUR darkies don't mean you ain't racist, it just mean you even MORE fucked-up! Shee-it, I been called a nigger in every major city in *(Name of country!)* And some a y'all think you bein' FRIENDLY by callin' me that!

And all a you people who consider yourselves to be "color-blind"? Y'all are the WORST mothafuckin' offenders. What is that shit? Color-blind. That's some bullshit right there.

*(He gestures to his face.)*

Does this look like a TAN to you, mothafucka?

Speakin' a tans, my docta told me I needed to exercise. Now, that gym shit freaks me the fuck out. All a them white folks hatin' theyselves for havin' a little bit a belly fat. Shit, black folks ain't like that. Once we past our skinny phase we just hurry up and get married so we don't have to worry 'bout that shit. "Pass me the mothafuckin' PORKCHOPS—I know I'M get-tin' pussy sometime next WEEK!"

*(He singles out an audience member with a knowing look.)*

And I might even get my asshole licked, too!

Naw, I can't handle the gym. What I like to do is run on rail-road tracks. For some reason, ever since I was a kid that's what I liked to do, is run on the railroad tracks. Now, the funny thing about railroad tracks, and this shit happens to me all the time, maybe it's happened to you—have you ever had the experi-ence where you standin' by a railroad track, and you hear the train comin', and you get a strong desire to step onto the rail-road track, get hit by the train, and die?

White people don't like to hear black people whine. They want black people to take some personal responsibility and shut the fuck up. But white people be some a the whininest mothafuckers out there! Seriously, you ever heard a white per-son whine? "I don't know what I'm doing with my life." "I hate feeling fat all the time." "Argh, I didn't get anything done today!" "That's reverse racism!"

And white folks always gotta be beastin'. Y'all know that term? "Beastin'"? Well, you can add it to your repertoire of semi-ironic hip-hop lingo. "Beastin'" is when I call you out on your racist bullshit and you turn around and say that I'M the one that's got the problem. THAT'S beastin', just bein' a beast. So I'm gonna say what I gotta say, and fuck it. If you don't like it, leave! This is MY show! If you don't like it, leave! A bunch a crackas stupid enough to give me a show, and my show is what they gon' get!

Oh yeah I said "cracka"! White people don't like it when they get called "cracka." They be like, "If I can't call you a nigger, then you can't call me a cracker." I like to call it the principle of "Even Steven." White people be all into Even Steven. The idea behind Even Steven is: If I got this much stuff *(He gestures high)* and you got this much stuff *(He gestures low)* and someone give us a cookie, then we gon' split that cookie EVENLY down the middle to be Even Steven. Now I'm not sayin' it's nice for me to go around callin' white people cracka, but the fact of the matter is that no one ever called anyone a cracka before lynchin' 'em. So take that, cracka! Whatchu gon' do?

So I been talkin' shit 'bout white folks for a while. Now it's time for me to go after some niggas. Black people be some of the stupidest, forty-drinkin', hot-wing-eatin', check-cashin', Tyler Perry–watchin', R. Kelly–listenin', dice-shootin', electric-slidin', money-mismanagin', Newport-smokin' mothafuckas in the WORLD.

Now, a lotta white folks in the audience just came.

*(He mimes jerking-off and coming while moaning the following:)*

Even Steven, Even Steven!

If I was to take a shit onstage, use my own shit as blackface paint, fuck a human brain until I came, suck my come back out of the brain, and spit it at the audience . . . I don't really know where I'm goin' with this.

Anyway, it ain't just white folks that's clueless. White, Asian, Latino, black. To be honest, I'm scared to walk into a room full a niggas! Anyone who ever seen me do an interview know I don't talk the same way onstage that I do in real life.

I even been accused a playin' a stereotype to cater to a white audience. Well, that's true, but mostly I talk this way because I'm fuckin' terrified a black people!

*(Imitating thug voice)* "Yo, who that nigga think he is, tryin' a sound like a white man an' shit! Let's fuck that nigga up!"

Shee-it! Bein' black can be fuckin' inconvenient! And white folks are always the ones who feel persecuted! I never met no black person who felt as persecuted as the white people I've met. Black people be like, "Man, fuck that shit!" and go about our business. See, we used to that shit! But for white people, the sense of persecution festers. They feel PERSECUTED when people call them out on their racism. That's like if I took a SHIT in yo FACE for three hundred years and then felt persecuted when you didn't swallow!

And in the event that you actually manage to convince a cracka that white privilege exists, they be like, "But what can I do? How can I get sick enough to make another person well?" Well I ain't advocating for any great political movement. And nobody expect you to feel guilty about slavery—you didn't do that shit! JUST ACKNOWLEDGE THE SYSTEMATIC RACISM THAT IS EMBEDDED IN OUR COUNTRY *(Outside the U.S.: "CULTURES")* AND TRY TO MAKE THINGS BETTER BY NOT CONSTANTLY ASKING ME TO PROVE THAT WHAT I EXPERI-ENCE IS REALLY RACISM OR REFERRING TO THE FACT THAT I'M BLACK OR MAKING ASSUMPTIONS ABOUT MY BACK-GROUND OR THE KIND OF MUSIC I LISTEN TO OR WHO I DATE, AND WHEN I CALL YOU OUT ON YOUR BULLSHIT, JUST FUCKING SAY I'M SORRY AND TRY NOT TO DO IT AGAIN! I know you think you treat black people the same way you do everyone else, but honestly you don't. You need to watch that subtle shit a little more carefully. Shit, I'm tired a dealin' with the cluelessness of white people, havin' to talk 'bout this race shit when I could be talkin' 'bout tiny pigs flyin' out my cock-hole or fairies that hatch in diarrhea.

*(He makes the poop face.)*

Speakin' a diarrhea, have you ever noticed how much shit comes outta newborn babies? People always makin' a fuss over babies like they the greatest thing on earth, when really they the worst fuckin' form a life known to man. Makin' you work for 'em twenty-four hours a day, lyin' there uselessly, shittin' theyselves and screamin'. I'm sorry, but fuck babies! Have you ever been tempted to make a baby stop cryin' by puttin' a pillow over its face and pressin' down till it can't breathe? Sometimes that's the only way!

My boner is hungry!

Old black folks be like, "Boy, wassa matta witch you? Why yo mouf got to be so dirty? Killin' babies ain't nothin' to laugh 'bout!" Well, I don't believe in taboos! I don't think it's wrong for people to fuck animals. Now, anyone who's ever had a pet knows animals can communicate—so if you some farmer foolin' 'round witch yo cow, and the cow seem into it, then that's some consensual shit right there!

The incest taboo offends me! Listen, if yo' sister want you to fuck her in the ass, and your dick hard, GO IN! Who gets hurt? I'm surprised more siblings don't fall in love! Shit, they got so much in common!

Anyway, now that I've cleansed your palates of all the angry race shit y'all don't wanna hear, lemme give you some more. I don't like it when you call me "brotha" or try and give me some kinda grip-down when I go to shake your hand. DON'T DO THAT SHIT! Also, don't say, "Oh, you must think I'm so white right now!" Shit, I LIKE it when white people act white! That ain't nothin' to be ashamed of—that's just keepin' it real.

And for all you white folks out there who walk on eggshells around black people, paranoid about sayin' the wrong thing that's gonna make us uncomfortable . . . shit, I like you. That's it. I like you. We black folks been doin' that shit for y'all since the day we got here! Keep up the good work! YOU my niggas. Peace out.

*(He starts to leave, comes back.)*

Oh, I almost forgot. For all you self-hating crackas who feel disappointed that I didn't sodomize you worse than I did—I got a white wife. She got blond hair, blue eyes, and BIG titties. She's also the most wonderful person I've ever known, and

I love her and my mixed tan babies more than anything in the world. Good night, *(Name of city!)*

*(Stand-Up Comedian exits as Mama and Rapper Omar enter.*
*Mama is wearing a long turquoise evening gown. She will also play Drug Dealer Mama, Video Ho, and Grandma from Heaven. Rapper Omar is wearing a black three-piece suit, white shirt, and red polka-dotted bow tie.*
*Mama stands and Rapper Omar lies flat on the floor.*
*In the following series of sketches, none of the performers should put on any kind of "black-sounding" or "white-sounding" accent. They should deliver their lines and move as flatly as possible. All props are mimed. They all wear visible wireless mikes. The performers should not hold for laughs until they get to the naturalistic play that closes the show.)*

MAMA: Omar wake up!
Wake up!
You have to go to school so that you can be a doctor!
RAPPER OMAR: I want to be a rap star!
MAMA: I worked three jobs and raised six children and ten grand-children by myself so that you could be a doctor!

*(He gets up to face her.)*

RAPPER OMAR: But rapping is my dream!
MAMA: I'm mad at you Omar!

*(He shrinks in the face of her wrath.)*

RAPPER OMAR: I'm sorry Mama.
MAMA: You won't do anything I want!
RAPPER OMAR: I just don't like school.
MAMA: Why?!
RAPPER OMAR: Because it's hard and it's boring and people shoot each other at my school!
MAMA: Maybe you should try hard like Frederick Douglass.
RAPPER OMAR: Mama, Frederick Douglass was a brain.
MAMA: I'm not interesting!

RAPPER OMAR: Don't say that Mama.

MAMA: I'm not interesting nobody is interested in me!
Why do you have to rap?!

RAPPER OMAR: Because rapping is fun and it sounds good and I can express myself.

MAMA: Okay I understand.
I'm proud of you for following your dreams.

*(Mama exits as Rapper Omar starts rapping. Sidekick Michael enters dribbling a basketball.*

*Sidekick Michael is played by the same actor who played Dancer 2 and is still wearing his black suit and flowered vest. The same actor will play Crackhead John, Bad Cop 2 and Sashay.*

*Rapper Omar "raps" by covering his mouth with his hand and swaying his hips from side to side while making clumsy "beatboxing" noises that sound like: "Puh, puh chuh. Puh, puh, puh chuh." Sidekick Michael "dribbles" by jerking his hand up and down flatly in rhythm with an imaginary basketball.)*

SIDEKICK MICHAEL: Hi Omar!

RAPPER OMAR: Hi Michael.

SIDEKICK MICHAEL: What are you doing?!

RAPPER OMAR: Practicing my rapping.

SIDEKICK MICHAEL: Hey check this out! Why did the turtle have no head?

RAPPER OMAR: I don't know. Why?

SIDEKICK MICHAEL: Because it got stuck in your butt!

*(He laughs a fake-sounding, hysterical laugh.)*

RAPPER OMAR: That wasn't funny.

SIDEKICK MICHAEL: Yes it was.

RAPPER OMAR: No it wasn't.

SIDEKICK MICHAEL: I'm funny!

RAPPER OMAR: Okay.

*(Pause.)*

SIDEKICK MICHAEL: Yo.

RAPPER OMAR: What.

SIDEKICK MICHAEL: Yo! Shit! Fuck! Goddamn!

RAPPER OMAR: Why are you swearing so much?

SIDEKICK MICHAEL: Because I'm crazy!

I'm going to go steal a car!

RAPPER OMAR: Why?

SIDEKICK MICHAEL: Because I'm sad.

RAPPER OMAR: Why are you sad?

SIDEKICK MICHAEL: Because my life is depressing.

RAPPER OMAR: I'm sorry Michael, but I don't think you should steal.

*(Grandpa Joe enters hobbling on his cane.*

*Grandpa Joe is played by the same actor who played the Stand-Up Comedian and is still wearing his black tux and skinny black tie. He will also play Bad Cop 1 and Paul the Extreme.)*

GRANDPA JOE: Did I hear you boys talking about stealing?

SIDEKICK MICHAEL: No, Grandpa Joe.

GRANDPA JOE: Back in my day—

*(Rapper Omar goes back to rapping and Sidekick Michael goes back to dribbling.)*

—stealing was considered wrong!

SIDEKICK MICHAEL: Hey, what's the difference between a testicle and a profiterole?!

GRANDPA JOE *(Pulling out a condom)*: Does either of you know what this is?

RAPPER OMAR: It's a condom.

GRANDPA JOE: That's right. And do you know what to do with it?

*(Sidekick Michael gets hit by stray machine-gun fire and dies.)*

RAPPER OMAR: Oh no! A drive-by shooting!

*(Rapper Omar runs offstage.)*

GRANDPA JOE *(Sadly)*: Nobody cares about what I have to say.

*(Grandpa Joe exits as Rapper Omar and Drug Dealer Desmond enter.*

*Drug Dealer Desmond is played by the same actor who played Dancer 1 and is still wearing his black tux and bow tie. He will also play Record Company Executive.)*

DRUG DEALER DESMOND: Hi Omar.
RAPPER OMAR: Hi Desmond.

*(Rapper Omar starts his "rapping." Drug Dealer Desmond starts making slight repetitive thuglike motions with his arms and shoulders that resemble the movements the characters in the video game* Grand Theft Auto *make when they are in their holding pattern. Periodically his arms will cross in front of him to complete the pattern before starting over again.)*

DRUG DEALER DESMOND: I'm going to rob people and shoot them and also sell drugs.
  You should do it, too.
RAPPER OMAR: But I don't want to be a drug dealer. I want to win this rap competition *(Pulls out flyer)* and get a recording contract.
DRUG DEALER DESMOND: But how are you going to get to the rap competition? You don't have a car or even money to buy bus fare.
RAPPER OMAR: That's a good point.
DRUG DEALER DESMOND: You could get the money by selling these drugs.

*(He holds out a packet of drugs.)*

RAPPER OMAR: I don't want to sell drugs!
DRUG DEALER DESMOND: Sell them!
RAPPER OMAR: No!
DRUG DEALER DESMOND: You better sell these drugs! Don't you want to be a rap star?
RAPPER OMAR *(Taking the drugs)*: Okay, but just this once.
DRUG DEALER DESMOND: Great.
  You're my best friend and I would die for you.
RAPPER OMAR: Me too.

DRUG DEALER DESMOND: I want to get a cat.

RAPPER OMAR: Why?

DRUG DEALER DESMOND: So I can cuddle with it.

RAPPER OMAR: I don't like cats.

DRUG DEALER DESMOND: But they're so nice and cuddly.

RAPPER OMAR: I don't like them they're from Satan.

DRUG DEALER DESMOND: You're from Satan!

RAPPER OMAR: No I'm not, I'm just allergic. And I don't like their evil eyes.

DRUG DEALER DESMOND: You have evil eyes!

RAPPER OMAR: You have evil eyes! You are actually evil because you just convinced me to sell drugs!

DRUG DEALER DESMOND: I just want a cat and a new gun and a bicycle to ride around the lake in France!

RAPPER OMAR: Is that your dream?

DRUG DEALER DESMOND: Yes.

RAPPER OMAR: That sounds like a white person's dream.

DRUG DEALER DESMOND: Well I am a white person.

RAPPER OMAR: How is that?

DRUG DEALER DESMOND: I just am. I'm white.

RAPPER OMAR: No you're not, you're black.

DRUG DEALER DESMOND: You're black.

RAPPER OMAR: You're black.

DRUG DEALER DESMOND: I can't remember which one of us is talking anymore.

RAPPER OMAR: You're the evil one and I'm the good one. Although now I'm evil too.

DRUG DEALER DESMOND: Cool! High-five!

*(They high-five—Rapper Omar unenthusiastically.)*

RAPPER OMAR: Now that you've ruined me, what will happen?

DRUG DEALER DESMOND: We're going to sell drugs and shoot anyone who gets in our way.

RAPPER OMAR: Why?

DRUG DEALER DESMOND: Because if you don't shoot people, then they don't respect you.

RAPPER OMAR: I need to learn more about the streets.

DRUG DEALER DESMOND: I will teach you.

*(Rapper Omar and Drug Dealer Desmond take a step forward to indicate that they are "on the streets.")*

Hey, do you want to buy some drugs?

RAPPER OMAR *(Waving his hand above his head)*: I have drugs! This sucks. Nobody wants to buy drugs from us.

DRUG DEALER DESMOND: I think something suspicious is going on. Usually everyone wants them.

RAPPER OMAR: What do you think is going on?

DRUG DEALER DESMOND: Let me investigate. Crackhead John!

*(Crackhead John enters. He enters in a straight line upstage of Rapper Omar and Drug Dealer Desmond, makes a sharp turn downstage, and lands crisply between them before slumping into his "Crackhead John" pose.)*

CRACKHEAD JOHN: Yes Desmond?

DRUG DEALER DESMOND: Crackhead John, do you know why nobody wants to buy our drugs?

CRACKHEAD JOHN: Yes. But what do I get in exchange?

DRUG DEALER DESMOND: Crack.

CRACKHEAD JOHN *(Pathetically)*: Yay!

RAPPER OMAR: Crackhead John, why isn't anyone buying our drugs?

CRACKHEAD JOHN: It's because there's a new drug dealer in town named Mama. And she told all the crackheads that if they bought drugs from anyone else, she'd shoot them in the face. And then one of them did buy drugs from someone else so Mama shot him in the face in front of everyone and said, "This is what will happen when you buy drugs from anyone else."

DRUG DEALER DESMOND: Where is this Mama? She's interfering with my business.

CRACKHEAD JOHN: Mama is on the corner of Grove and Elm.

DRUG DEALER DESMOND: Thank you, Crackhead John. Here is some crack for you.

CRACKHEAD JOHN *(Pathetically)*: Yay!

*(Crackhead John exits.)*

RAPPER OMAR *(Looking after Crackhead John)*: Crack is bad.

DRUG DEALER DESMOND: I don't care I like it.

RAPPER OMAR: Maybe we shouldn't sell crack.

DRUG DEALER DESMOND: You know what's bad?

RAPPER OMAR: What.

DRUG DEALER DESMOND: Caffeine.

RAPPER OMAR: Caffeine isn't bad!

DRUG DEALER DESMOND: Caffeine is really bad!

RAPPER OMAR: Here's your crack Desmond I'm not selling it!

DRUG DEALER DESMOND: But then how are you going to get to the rap competition?

RAPPER OMAR: Oh yeah that's right I forgot.

DRUG DEALER DESMOND: You're a pussy.

RAPPER OMAR: I don't like that!

DRUG DEALER DESMOND: You're a pussy who doesn't want to sell drugs!

RAPPER OMAR: Shut up Desmond you're mean!

DRUG DEALER DESMOND: I am mean! I'm the meanest there is! And I'm going to find that Mama and shoot her in the tit-tays!

*(Drug Dealer Mama enters. She, like Desmond, moves in a* Grand Theft Auto–*style holding pattern, only her arms cross higher than Desmond's.)*

Hey, Mama!

DRUG DEALER MAMA: I'm going to shoot you both in the face!

DRUG DEALER DESMOND: Not before I shoot you first!

DRUG DEALER MAMA: I'm going to shoot you before you can shoot me!

DRUG DEALER DESMOND: I'd like to see you try!

*(They shoot at each other and miss.)*

RAPPER OMAR: Guys, guys! Isn't there some way to settle this without shooting each other?

DRUG DEALER DESMOND AND DRUG DEALER MAMA: NO!

DRUG DEALER MAMA: All I want is for everyone to stay off my corners and keep their drugs to themselves!

DRUG DEALER DESMOND: I have customers, and those customers need drugs, and I have drugs to sell! If you shoot my customers in the face for buying drugs from me, then that makes me mad!

DRUG DEALER MAMA: Look at it from my point of view! I'm new in town and don't have any customers! So I need to steal yours!

DRUG DEALER DESMOND: THAT MAKES ME ANGRY!

RAPPER OMAR: It is a seemingly insoluble dilemma.

DRUG DEALER MAMA: I can solve it by shooting you in the face!

DRUG DEALER DESMOND: Not if I shoot you first!

*(They shoot each other in the face and collapse on the floor at awkward angles.)*

RAPPER OMAR: Desmond! My best friend Desmond! This is a tragedy!

*(Bad Cop 1 and Bad Cop 2 enter.)*

BAD COP 1: What's going on!

RAPPER OMAR: Desmond Desmond!

BAD COP 2: I don't like black people.

RAPPER OMAR: But you're black!

BAD COP 2: No I'm not.

BAD COP 1 *(Pointing at Rapper Omar)*: I arrest you!

RAPPER OMAR: For what?

BAD COP 1 *(Pulling out a packet of drugs)*: For dealing these drugs.

RAPPER OMAR *(Pulling out his packet of drugs)*: But I only have these many!

BAD COP 1 *(Shaking his packet of drugs)*: Now you have THESE many.

RAPPER OMAR: That's not fair! I have to compete in a rap competition!

BAD COP 2: Rap is for ANIMALS! Your life is over!

*(The Bad Cops take Rapper Omar by each arm and push him onto the floor.*

*Rapper Omar sits cross-legged, looking traumatized. Bad Cop 1 turns into Paul the Extreme and stands upstage right of Rapper Omar.)*

PAUL THE EXTREME: Hey kid.

Hey kid are you deaf or are you mad because you're in prison?

RAPPER OMAR: Leave me alone. My anus is all stretched-out already. You wouldn't like it.

PAUL THE EXTREME: Hey kid what's your name?

RAPPER OMAR: Omar. But my anus is all stretched-out.

PAUL THE EXTREME: I do not have relations with the anus of a man.

RAPPER OMAR: That's good.

PAUL THE EXTREME: My name is Paul the Extreme.

RAPPER OMAR: What do you want from me?

PAUL THE EXTREME: I want to teach you.

RAPPER OMAR: I don't want to be brainwashed by your religion. I'm a Christian.

PAUL THE EXTREME: Christianity is the white man's filth religion. My religion is the only true way for the black man. Here is my book of religion.

RAPPER OMAR: It's written in gobbledygook!

PAUL THE EXTREME: I will teach you.

RAPPER OMAR: But I don't want to learn.

PAUL THE EXTREME: You have to!

RAPPER OMAR: No!

PAUL THE EXTREME: Why are you doing this to me?

RAPPER OMAR: I just don't feel like learning anything right now!

PAUL THE EXTREME: That makes me cry.

*(He cries.)*

RAPPER OMAR: Don't cry, Mr. Extreme.

PAUL THE EXTREME *(Crying)*: You made me cry!

RAPPER OMAR: Please stop!

*(Paul the Extreme cries harder.)*

Okay I'll learn your religion.

PAUL THE EXTREME: Great.

*(He opens his book of religion and shows a page to Rapper Omar.)*

Saints are getting the tops of their heads sawed off, and the people are laughing. Then they realize they have not been chosen. They are looking back in fear. The angels are all at the top. The people are also elevated. Suddenly something changes. Who are these people? It's actually the pope first. Following the pope, the emperor. Following the emperor, the king. Following the king are the religious people. Following the religious people are the wealthy. There are butterflies flying out of my palms, thanks to our bishop. I need to go away from here. I am longing for a life that is somewhere else. Who made this? *(Accusingly)* Italian *(Pronounced "Eye-talian")* people.

RAPPER OMAR: I don't understand.

PAUL THE EXTREME: I hate white people.

RAPPER OMAR: Why?

PAUL THE EXTREME: Because they are mean.

RAPPER OMAR: Oh.

PAUL THE EXTREME: With so many white people running loose on the streets, why do we point our gun barrels at each other?

RAPPER OMAR: I don't know.

PAUL THE EXTREME: We should shoot the white people instead.

RAPPER OMAR: That's a good idea.

PAUL THE EXTREME: Omar, what is your greatest wish?

RAPPER OMAR: To be a rap star.

PAUL THE EXTREME: Then you must go forth and rap about killing white people until there are no white people left.

RAPPER OMAR: Okay.

*(Rapper Omar walks upstage and turns to face downstage as the other performers run onstage and sit cross-legged facing him, forming an audience of prisoners.)*

Fellow prisoners! I rap for you!

*(He does his accustomed "rapping" gesture and sound.)*

Puh, puh chuh. Puh, puh, puh chuh.
Puh, puh chuh. Puh, puh, puh chuh.

*(Getting more intense:)*

Puh, puh chuh. Puh, puh, puh chuh!

*(Getting really intense:)*

PUH, PUH CHUH. PUH, PUH, PUH CHUH!

I'm the master rapper and I'm here to say
I hate white people in a major way
Whitey honky cracka, I wish you were dead
To get that fruity taste I gotta shoot you in the head!

*(All the prisoners cheer and run off except for Record Company Executive, who approaches Omar.)*

RECORD COMPANY EXECUTIVE: Yo, I'm a record company executive and when we both get out of here in two months, I'm going to make you a star!
RAPPER OMAR: I can't believe it!

*(Record Company Executive exits. Sashay enters, bringing a black cube downstage that Rapper Omar sits on.)*

SASHAY: Do you want your hair like this or like this for the video?
RAPPER OMAR: I don't know.
SASHAY: Sashay thinks you should wear your hair like this.
RAPPER OMAR: Who is Sashay?
SASHAY: Who is Sashay?

*(He sings and dances awkwardly to the tune of the* Jem and the Holograms *theme song.)*

Sashay! (Sashay is excitement!)
Ooh Sashay! (Sashay is adventure!) Ooh!
Glamour and glitter
Fashion and fame

Sashay! Sashay is truly outrageous
Truly, truly, truly outrageous
Oh whoa Sashay! (Sashay!)
The music's contagious! (Outrageous!)

Sashay is my name
No one else is the same
Sashay is my name!

Sashay!

RAPPER OMAR: Nice to meet you, Sashay.

SASHAY: Omar, would you like to go on a date with me?

RAPPER OMAR: No thank you, I'm married to a woman.

SASHAY: Let me convert you! Being gay is fun!

*(He makes a "being gay is fun" gesture.
    Video Ho enters.)*

VIDEO HO: Hi Omar.

RAPPER OMAR: Hi Video Ho.

VIDEO HO: Do you like my booty?

RAPPER OMAR: Yes.

VIDEO HO: Do you like my boobs?

RAPPER OMAR: Yes.

VIDEO HO: I like expensive things.

RAPPER OMAR: Okay.

VIDEO HO: I'll meet you in your trailer in fifteen minutes.

RAPPER OMAR: Okay.

*(Video Ho lifts one hand high over her head and snaps her fingers.
    Then she leans menacingly toward Rapper Omar and exits.)*

SASHAY: Ooh, Omar. You are truly truly truly outrageous!

*(Rapper Omar does five lines of coke, then shoots up.)*

That's a lot of drugs.

RAPPER OMAR: I need a lot.

SASHAY: Why do you need so many?

RAPPER OMAR: Because I'm addicted.

VIDEO HO *(Shouting from offstage)*: Omar, get in here and do stuff to my booty!

*(Rapper Omar sighs.)*

RAPPER OMAR: I better go.

SASHAY: Good luck, Omar! I wish you'd converted. I'm a really nice boyfriend.

*(Sashay exits and Rapper Omar addresses the black cube as if it were a gravestone:)*

RAPPER OMAR: Oh Desmond. If only you were here to see me now, in my fur coat, gold chains, and designer sunglasses.

Here I am, with all of my dreams come true, but now my mortality presses upon me and death approaches fast.

I was happier in prison with Paul the Extreme!

I'm tired of eating a different pussy every night. I'm tired of being on drugs all the time. I'm on drugs right now!

It's so boring. I'm bored!

And being famous isn't as good as I thought it was going to be. I have to do all this stuff I don't want to do, like sign autographs until my hand hurts.

I feel that there is nothing to live for except drugs and sex and unhealthy foods. Oh Desmond, I don't even have any friends anymore because I fucked all their wives and girlfriends.

*(He gets on his knees downstage of the cube.)*

Dear Lord, I am praying to you now. Please shine down from Heaven and show me the way. I have grown to hate the very rap that I once loved. Sometimes I don't even feel like taking a shower!

Please Lord, show me the way!

*(Grandma from Heaven enters and stands on the cube behind Rapper Omar. He turns to face her.)*

GRANDMA FROM HEAVEN: Here is a parable from me, Grandma from Heaven:

There were two cranes. And the first crane had one red berry for an eye, which the second crane pecked out and ate. And that berry expanded to the size of a world inside the greedy crane until its crane-flesh burst open and went flying in every direction. And that world-sized berry developed boils the shape of a people, which were red and hungry, and which fed upon each other until the juice was dripping down everyone's faces. And the people walked around with parts of their bodies missing—chunks of ear, a bite out of their backs. And the crane that had been eviscerated began to gather up all its molecules to re-form feathers and flesh and eyes and beak, until it found itself whole and healthy on a planet of red berry earth and flesh. And the crane gorged itself until it was as round and red as the planet itself. And everyone sat around, crippled and maimed and feeding, until the sun went down.

*(Rapper Omar helps Grandma from Heaven off the cube and they become Singer 2 and Singer 1, respectively. The actor who played Drug Dealer Desmond enters as Singer 3.*

*They stand in a line looking around at the audience in silence. They look at the audience for an uncomfortably long time.*

*As they sing an a cappella rendition of the indie-rock song "Dark Center of the Universe" by Modest Mouse, they continue to look around at the audience. They don't move or change expression, but they sing with feeling.)*

SINGER 1 *(Singing)*:
I might disintegrate into the thin air if you'd like
I'm not the dark center of the universe like you thought

SINGERS 1, 2 AND 3 *(In unison)*:

I might disintegrate into the thin air if you'd like
I'm not the dark center of the universe like you thought

*(In three-part harmony:)*

Well, it took a lot of work to be the ass I am
And I'm real damn sure that anyone can, equally easily fuck
    you over
Well, died sayin' something, but I didn't mean it
Everyone's life ends, no one ever completes it
Dry or wet ice, they both melt and you're equally cheated

Well, it took a lot of work to be the ass I am
And I'm real damn sure that anyone can, equally easily fuck
    you over
Well, an endless ocean landin' on an endless desert

Well, it's funny as hell, but no one laughs when they get there
If you can't see the thin air then why the hell should you care?

Well, it took a lot of work to be the ass I am
And I'm real damn sure that anyone can, equally easily fuck
    you over
Well, I'm sure you'd tell me you got nothing to say
But our voices shook hands the other day
If you can't see the thin air what the hell is in the way?

*(The three-part harmony gets more complex:)*

I might disintegrate into the thin air if you'd like
I'm not the dark center of the universe like you thought

Well, it took a lot of work to be the ass I am
And I'm real damn sure that anyone can, equally easily fuck
    you over
Well, an endless ocean landin' on an endless desert
Well, it's funny as hell, but no one laughs when they get there
If you can't see the thin air then why the hell should you care?

Well, it took a lot of work to be the ass I am
And I'm real damn sure that anyone can, equally easily fuck
    you over
Well, died sayin' something, but I didn't mean it
Everyone's life ends, no one ever completes it
Dry or wet ice, they both melt and you're equally cheated

Well, it took a lot of work to be the ass I am
And I'm real damn sure that anyone can, equally easily fuck
    you over
Well, I'm sure you'll tell me you got nothin' to say
But our voices shook hands the other day
If you can't see the thin air then what the hell is in your way?

*(The Singers exit as Mary J. Blige's soul/pop song "Ooh" begins.
    Stagehand 1 and Stagehand 2 enter carrying dollies. They are both
white males over the age of fifty, wearing blue jeans. Stagehand 1 wears
a lilac hooded sweatshirt and Stagehand 2 wears a blue T-shirt.*

*They wheel out a brown leather couch with a large rug rolled up on
top of it. They set down the couch and roll out the rug. They bring on
a long coffee table/book shelf that contains books and a baseball in a
glass case. Then, a wooden folding chair, a lamp, a stacked side table,
a rolling bar cart, and a black leather side chair. They carry on a vase
with a ridiculously phallic flower arrangement in it. Then, a plate of
salami, crackers and cheese. Also, a bowl of nuts, napkins, and chips
and salsa. Everything looks modern, expensive and masculine.*

*The Stagehands grab their dollies and exit offstage right as
Thomas and Omar enter stage left.*

*Thomas is played by the actor who played the Stand-Up Come-
dian. Omar is played by the actor who played Sashay. Desmond is
played by the actor who played Drug Dealer Desmond. Thomasina
is played by the actor who played Mama. Michael is played by the
actor who played Rapper Omar.*

*Omar wears the same black suit/flowered vest/white shoes combo
he wore at the top of the show. Thomas is now wearing a three-piece,
charcoal pin-striped suit with a white shirt and striped tie.*

*Thomas and Omar sit on the couch. They look tense and awkward.)*

THOMAS: What about eggs.

OMAR: Yes, I eat eggs.

THOMAS: But no dairy.

OMAR: No dairy and no meat. But I'll eat fish.

THOMAS: Just fish or all seafood.

OMAR: All seafood.

THOMAS: Do you eat butter?

OMAR: It's interesting that you would ask me that, because I was eating butter for a while but then I switched to olive oil. Did you
know that you can put olive oil on toast?

*(Pause.)*

THOMAS: What about alcohol.

OMAR: Oh, no! No alcohol, tobacco, drugs, caffeine, sugar, meat,
dairy, salt, refined grains . . . I think that's it.

THOMAS *(Gesturing at the coffee table)*: I don't think there's anything
here for you to eat. The last time I saw you, you seemed to be
eating mostly bacon and potato chips.

*(Omar flinches.)*

Are you sure I can't get you anything to drink? Cranberry juice and seltzer?

OMAR: Uh . . . I'm still on the fence about the whole juice thing. Maybe later.

THOMAS: Plain seltzer?

OMAR: Actually I used to drink four liters of seltzer a day until someone told me it hollows out your bones.

THOMAS: Hollows out your bones?

OMAR: They said that drinking seltzer hollows out your bones.

THOMAS: That can't be right.

OMAR: I don't know.

THOMAS: I love seltzer.

OMAR: Me too. But hollow bones . . .

THOMAS: That can't be right. I wish you hadn't told me that, Omar.

OMAR: I'm sorry, but don't you want to know? So you can stop drinking it?

THOMAS: I don't want to stop drinking it. I want to drink as much of it as I want whenever I want without worrying about whether or not it's going to hollow out my bones!

OMAR: I'm sorry, Thomas. Maybe it's not even true. You should look it up on the internet.

THOMAS *(Snapping)*: People are always telling me to look things up on the internet, but when am I ever going to have the time?
Last night I drank an entire bottle of maple syrup.

OMAR: What?

THOMAS: Every night before I go to sleep I drink a bottle of maple syrup and then I eat three candy bars in a row.

OMAR: You can't be serious.

THOMAS: Yes I eat three candy bars in a row and then go to bed without brushing my teeth.

OMAR: How come all your teeth haven't fallen out?

THOMAS: I don't know. I haven't been to a dentist in over eight years.

*(Omar looks disgusted.*
*Pause.)*

OMAR: What time is it?

THOMAS: 7:30.

OMAR: Huh.

THOMAS: What.

OMAR: Did you invite a lot of people?

THOMAS: A few.

OMAR: Hm.

THOMAS: It's only 7:30. You came at seven right on the dot.

OMAR: I like to be on time.

THOMAS: I know, you came right on the dot at seven.

OMAR: I hate it when people are late. I hate waiting for people.

THOMAS: I don't mind waiting. Sometimes I meet people. Sometimes people just come up to me and strike up a conversation. I love it.

OMAR: I don't like it when people speak to me in public. Strangers. Like on a airplane. When I'm on an airplane I try to emit a force field of unfriendliness so that no one will speak to me, and it works.

I don't like parties, I don't like talking to lots of people. Even if it's all people I like, it stresses me out to see their faces. To see everyone's face all at once. It stresses me out.

THOMAS: You're at a party now.

OMAR: No, I like parties. But I prefer one-on-one. Definitely I'm better at one-on-one.

*(Sound of a buzzer.)*

THOMAS: Oh, someone's here. I'll be right back.

*(He exits.*

*Omar practices different ways of sitting, trying to find one that looks cool.*

*Thomas reenters with Desmond, who is wearing the same black tux/cummerbund/bow tie outfit he wore at the top of the show.)*

Desmond, this is Omar. Omar, Desmond.

OMAR: Nice to meet you.

*(Desmond doesn't respond.)*

THOMAS: Can I get you something to drink? I can get you a scotch, cranberry and vodka, gin and tonic, rum and Coke, beer, wine.

DESMOND: I'll have a tequila sunrise, please.

*(Thomas looks taken aback.*
*Desmond goes to the leather side chair and sits.)*

THOMAS: Uh, I'll be right back.

*(Thomas exits.*
*Pause.)*

OMAR: So how do you know Thomas?

DESMOND *(Looking at Omar expressionlessly and then turning away)*: We work together.

OMAR: Do you live around here?

DESMOND: No.

OMAR: Are you married?

DESMOND: Yes.

OMAR: Do you have any children?

DESMOND: No.

OMAR: Why not?

DESMOND: Because I don't want any.

*(Thomas reenters with tequila and starts making drinks.)*

THOMAS: So, Desmond, how are things with you?

DESMOND: Fine.

THOMAS: I heard things got a little sticky for you the other day.

DESMOND *(Sharply)*: Who told you that?

THOMAS: Thomasina.

DESMOND: Thomasina told you that things got a little sticky for me the other day?

THOMAS: She didn't go into detail, she just mentioned it lightly, in passing.

DESMOND: Is Thomasina coming here tonight?

THOMAS: I invited her.

OMAR: Who's Thomasina?

THOMAS: Thomasina is our friend from work.

Desmond, I didn't mean to offend you. I didn't know it was all so serious.

DESMOND *(Very seriously)*: It's not serious. It's not serious at all.

THOMAS: Here's a tequila sunrise for you, and a cranberry juice without seltzer for you.

OMAR *(Panicky)*: Oh no thank you. I don't feel like drinking anything right now!

THOMAS *(Irritated)*: Well at least let me put it in front of you in case you get thirsty later.

OMAR: All right.

DESMOND: What is this?

THOMAS: It's a tequila sunrise.

DESMOND: It doesn't taste like a tequila sunrise.

THOMAS: What does it taste like?

DESMOND: It tastes like iodine.

THOMAS: Well I don't have any iodine in the house so I don't know why it would taste like that. It's just tequila and orange juice and little bit of grenadine. Maybe it's the grenadine. I buy the generic brand.

OMAR: I always buy generic! Everything in my house is generic! I never buy name brands, ever!

DESMOND: I don't think it's the grenadine.

THOMAS: Well I don't know what it could be, then. It's good tequila. Do you want me to fix you something else?

DESMOND: No.

*(Pause.)*

THOMAS: Desmond, do you want to take a look at that thing I was talking about?

DESMOND: I don't think so.

THOMAS: But that thing—I thought you wanted . . .

Do you want to go look at that thing?

DESMOND: Oh!

All right.

THOMAS: Omar would you excuse us for a minute? We'll be right back.

OMAR: Sure.

*(Thomas and Desmond exit hurriedly.*

*Omar stands up and paces around. He stares at the food on the coffee table. He puts his face very close to the food and starts inhaling deeply and trying to waft the scent toward his nose with his hands. He starts sucking at the air above the food in a disturbing way.*

*Thomasina and Michael enter and stare at Omar.*

*Thomasina is wearing a champagne-colored satin cocktail dress with a princess skirt. Michael is wearing brown pants and a tweed jacket with elbow patches. Under the jacket he wears a blue button-down shirt, brown V-neck sweater, and tie.)*

THOMASINA: Hello.

OMAR *(Startled)*: Hi. How did you get in?

THOMASINA: The door was open. Is Thomas here?

OMAR: He's in the other room doing coke with Desmond.

*(Thomasina and Michael exchange looks.)*

THOMASINA: I'm Thomasina, and this is Michael.

OMAR: Hi, I'm Omar.

MICHAEL: Nice to meet you, Omar.

*(They sit awkwardly.)*

*(To Omar)* You know, it's funny, but you look just like my cousin Freddy.

OMAR: Really?

MICHAEL: Yeah, you two even dress the same. Very stylish.

THOMASINA: It's true. I love your vest, Omar.

OMAR: Thank you!!!

MICHAEL: I've never been able to understand how stylish people can be so stylish.

THOMASINA: What are you talking about Michael, you dress really well!

MICHAEL: Anyone can go out and buy a jacket, but I would never be able to put together an outfit like that. That kind of thing requires an artistic eye.

OMAR: I don't know what to say!!!

THOMASINA: Oh Omar, you're embarrassed. That's so cute!

OMAR: Hey, would you two like to come watch the Oscars at my house this Sunday?

*(Pause.)*

THOMASINA: Uhh . . .

MICHAEL: Uhh . . . let me check my calendar.

*(He reluctantly checks his calendar.)*

It looks like I'm free that evening, so . . .

OMAR: Great!

THOMASINA: Michael I'm so excited for you to meet Thomas.

MICHAEL: Me too.

THOMASINA: I'm sorry I've been so busy.

MICHAEL: Oh, don't even worry about it.

THOMASINA: How's Shannon?

MICHAEL *(Unconvincingly)*: She's fine.

*(Thomasina gives him a look.)*

We've been having some problems.

OMAR: Really? What kind of problems?

THOMASINA: You don't have to tell us anything, Michael.

MICHAEL: No, it's not a big deal, I don't mind talking about it. It's just we got into a big fight the other day.

OMAR: Mm, what happened?

MICHAEL: Well, we were having a conversation about our exes . . .

THOMASINA: Augh, why?

MICHAEL: I don't know, because we're idiots. And she admitted that if her ex Paul who broke her heart were to hit on her again, she would feel tempted to sleep with him.

OMAR: What?!

THOMASINA: You mean Paul from her work Paul?

MICHAEL: The Paul whom she sees every day, goes on business trips with, and talks to constantly on the phone.

OMAR: Fuck!!!

THOMASINA: What did you do?

MICHAEL: I got really upset and walked out, and didn't call her for like a day, but then she called and I picked up.

THOMASINA: What did she say?

MICHAEL: Well, that's the thing. I wanted her to apologize and say something reassuring, like, "I love you and you're so much better than Paul is and have a way bigger cock," but instead she was like, "Michael, I'm *with you*. What I'm talking about is purely sexual. I would feel that way about *any* of my exes."

OMAR: That's really really really fucked-up!!!

MICHAEL: And then I felt like a jealous freak, so I was like, "Okay, I understand."

THOMASINA: Michael, I know I'm not supposed to do this, but I'm going to be really honest with you.

MICHAEL: Shit.

THOMASINA: You deserve better than this, Michael. You are like the world's most perfect boyfriend and this behavior you're describing is completely shitty and unacceptable.

MICHAEL: I know she's difficult, but she's like a genius. If we broke up I don't think I could find anyone better than her.

THOMASINA: Now Michael, you know I will support you in anything you do, but honey I'm telling you that there is someone out there for you whom you can be madly in love with and who won't do fucked-up things to you.

OMAR: Michael, I want to be honest with you as well. Shannon isn't doing anything to you. You're doing it all to yourself.

MICHAEL: I beg your pardon?

OMAR: Michael, I want you to go home and write down a list of every nasty thing Shannon has ever done to you, and then cross out each instance of the word "Shannon" and replace it with the word "I."

MICHAEL: Are you joking?

*(Thomas and Desmond reenter.)*

THOMAS: Hey, you're here! Sorry, I was just showing Desmond something.

THOMASINA: Oh, that's all right. We were all just getting acquainted. Thomas and Desmond, this is Michael. Michael, Thomas and Desmond.

THOMAS *(To Michael)*: It's nice to finally meet you!

MICHAEL: It's nice to meet you, too! *(To Desmond)* Hey, what's up.

DESMOND *(Coldly)*: Hi.

THOMAS: Can I get you guys something to drink? I have cranberry and vodka, rum and Coke, gin and tonic, wine, beer . . . I can make a martini.

THOMASINA: I'm okay. I've been trying not to drink so much lately.

MICHAEL: Really? Me too!

THOMASINA: No way! Isn't it amazing how much better you feel?

MICHAEL: It's great!

THOMASINA: I'm even considering going to AA. All of my friends go and they love it.

MICHAEL: I've been thinking I should go to AA too!

THOMASINA: We should go together!

MICHAEL: What's your schedule like next week?

THOMAS: WHAT IS WRONG WITH EVERYONE?

OMAR: There's nothing wrong with not wanting to be an alcoholic.

THOMAS: Who said anything about being an alcoholic?

    Okay. Here's what's going to happen.

*(He gets glasses and pours scotch.)*

I'm going to pour everyone a double shot of scotch and every-one here is going to drink it down. Including you, Omar.

OMAR: Thomas, I really can't! My system is hypersensitive to stim-ulants of any kind.

THOMAS: Fuck you, Omar, you're drinking.

*(Thomas pours.)*

THOMASINA: Is everything all right, Thomas?

THOMAS: I'm fine! It's just that this is a party and everyone has to drink! I'm sick of this bullshit.

*(Desmond takes a glass, oblivious. Everyone else stares unhappily at the glasses on the table while Thomas glares at them threateningly.)*

THOMASINA *(Reluctantly)*: All right then, let's drink.

MICHAEL: This is an awfully nice scotch.

OMAR: Thomas, I am telling you right now that if I drink any of that I'm going to fall into a very deep depression starting tomorrow.

THOMAS: Omar, do you really want to be the only person at this party who's not drinking?

*(Omar looks around at everyone. Everyone stares back at him. He snatches up the glass angrily and walks away from the group.)*

I didn't think so.

*(Thomas lifts his glass.)*

To alcohol! Alcohol, I love you. I love the way you look in the glass, so amber and exquisite. I love the way you feel sliding down my throat. I love the numbness that you bring.
Cheers!

*(Everyone looks weirded-out except for Desmond, who acts as if this were a normal toast.)*

EVERYONE ELSE: Cheers.

*(Everyone drinks. Omar goes to sit next to Thomasina on the couch but Desmond blocks him with his foot and takes the seat himself.)*

THOMASINA: So Desmond, what were you holed up with Charlie about for so long today?

DESMOND: I beg your pardon?

THOMASINA: Was it about the Hopkins account?

DESMOND: I don't know what you're referring to.

THOMASINA: What do you mean?

*(Desmond laughs hysterically. Thomasina stares at him.)*

THOMAS: Everyone, I would like to make an announcement!

*(Everyone looks at Thomas.)*

THOMAS: Today is my birthday.

THOMASINA: Happy birthday, Thomas! I wish you'd told me!

OMAR: I totally forgot. I feel terrible.

MICHAEL: Happy birthday, Thomas.

DESMOND: Happy birthday.

THOMAS: Today I am thirty years old.

THOMASINA: Wow, that's huge!

*(Thomas exits suddenly.)*

MICHAEL: Where did he go? Do you think he's okay?

THOMASINA: Why wouldn't he be okay?

MICHAEL: Is this how he usually acts?

THOMASINA: He's fine. He's just a little tipsy. Right Omar?

OMAR: I don't know. I haven't seen him in a long time. I don't really know what he's like these days.

MICHAEL: I think he's acting weird.

THOMASINA: Oh Michael, you act like you've never seen a drunk person before.

*(Thomas reenters with a cheap-looking birthday cake with one big lit candle in the shape of the number thirty.)*

THOMAS *(Singing loudly, as the others awkwardly join in)*: Happy birthday to me! Happy birthday to me! Happy birthday dear Thomas! Happy birthday to me!
*(Shouting)* Yeah!

*(He pauses to make a wish and blows out the candle.)*

THOMASINA: Should I get a knife and—

THOMAS: No!

*(Thomas pulls the candle out of the cake, sucks the frosting off, and throws it on the floor.*
*He sticks his finger in the frosting and licks the frosting off. He digs into the cake with his fingers and starts eating it with his hand.)*

OMAR: Thomas are you drunk?

THOMAS: No.

OMAR: Thomasina thinks you are.

THOMAS: Thomasina, did you say I was drunk?

THOMASINA: No, Thomas, I did not.

OMAR: You're lying! She's lying, Thomas! Michael, didn't Thomasina say she thought Thomas was drunk?

MICHAEL: Uh . . .

THOMASINA: Omar, you're being ridiculous.

OMAR: I'm not being ridiculous. You lied! To everyone's face!

MICHAEL: Hey, does anyone want to play Library?

OMAR: What's Library?

DESMOND: It's an extremely boring game.

OMAR: How does it go?

DESMOND: It's too boring even to describe.

OMAR: You know what I hate more than anything in the world is when someone says, "Let's play a game," and then people use it as an excuse to do mean things to each other.

THOMASINA: Library isn't that type of game, Omar. I love Library!

DESMOND: I would like to play Library.

*(Everyone stares at Desmond.*
*Thomas gets a glint in his eye.)*

THOMAS: Thomasina, how is Jonathan's new book coming?

THOMASINA: I think it's going well. He works on it all the time.

DESMOND: Who's Jonathan?

THOMASINA: Jonathan is my boyfriend.

THOMAS: How are things with you two?

THOMASINA: Great. Really, really good.

*(Thomas starts snickering.)*

Thomas?

*(Thomas cracks up.)*

You want to tell us what's so funny?

THOMAS *(Cracking up)*: Have you gotten to the plastic sheet phase yet?

OMAR: What's the plastic sheet phase?

MICHAEL: Thomas—

THOMAS: When Thomasina gets serious about a guy, she has to bust out the plastic sheets.

OMAR: Why, does she wet the bed or something?

*(Horrible pause.)*

THOMASINA: Fuck you, Thomas.

Who else have you told? Does everyone at work know?

THOMAS: No.

THOMASINA *(Getting up)*: You know what? Jonathan does have plastic sheets on his bed. Because he loves me. But you wouldn't know anything about that, would you Thomas?

THOMAS: You know who else loves you? Desmond.

THOMASINA: What?

THOMAS: Desmond, you're in love with Thomasina, right?

DESMOND: Yes.

OMAR *(Pointing at Desmond)*: But you're married!

DESMOND: My wife is leaving me for another man.

THOMASINA: Well, I'm terribly sorry to hear that, Desmond, but I'm in a serious relationship.

THOMAS: Why don't you tell her how you feel, Desmond?

DESMOND: I feel . . . all the time, I think about what I'm going to wear. To work. Where you will see me. Where you will see me and what I'm wearing. All the time I think about that. I think about my shoes. I think about my tie. I imagine you seeing my shoes and my tie at work. I can't wait to see you. When you go on vacation, I wait for you to come back. I wait all the time. Sometimes you and Thomas go to lunch. One time I heard you sing, as a joke.

THOMASINA: Desmond, that was so . . . I don't know how to respond.

THOMAS: I guess you're gonna need more plastic sheets.

THOMASINA: What the hell is wrong with you, Thomas? You think being an asshole makes you a man? You're a cowardly little prick who failed at baseball and lives like a child! It's no wonder none of my friends want to date you.

*(Pause.)*

I'm sorry, that was mean.

DESMOND: It's fine! Thomas is a bad person!

THOMASINA: Thomas is not a bad person! I don't understand why he's doing this.

THOMAS: Omar is a virgin.

OMAR: I am not!

THOMAS: Well that's what you told me.

OMAR: I didn't! You're lying! He's lying!

THOMAS: So you've had sex?

OMAR: Yes!

THOMAS: Oh boy. What was *that* like?

OMAR: It was fine.

THOMAS: Oh yeah, who'd you fuck?

OMAR: I don't have to tell you that!

THOMAS: You won't tell me because the person doesn't exist.

OMAR: That isn't true!

THOMAS: Come on Omar, you're a virgin!

OMAR: I hate you, Thomas.

THOMAS: It's not my fault that you're a LIAR, Omar!

OMAR: I'M NOT A LIAR! I'M NOT A LIAR!

THOMASINA: Omar, calm down, it's okay. No one here thinks you're a liar.

THOMAS: Omar's not stupid, Thomasina. He knows we all think he's a BIG FAT LIAR.

DESMOND: Stop it, Thomas!

THOMAS: Fuck you, Desmond. You're a liar, too. I know what you told Charlie in his office today.

DESMOND *(Afraid)*: I didn't.

THOMAS: You're a bad person, Desmond.

DESMOND: No.

OMAR: Thomas, I'm glad. I'm glad you're doing this. Because ever since we were kids, you've been mean, and nobody knew it but me. Now everyone knows! I'm going home.

THOMASINA: Omar.

*(He gets up.)*

OMAR: I know that people don't like me. It's always been like that. But I don't know how to be any other way. If I could sign up for a class to change myself, I . . .

Thomas, you've always had so many friends, and this is how you treat them. It makes no sense.

It was nice meeting all of you.

THOMASINA: No one here dislikes you Omar. I think we should all go get a drink and leave Thomas here to be an asshole by himself.

THOMAS: I have a second announcement to make!

*(Everyone looks at him.)*

I poisoned all of your drinks!

*(It should be clear from this point on that nobody believes Thomas poisoned them, with the exception of Desmond. Thomasina, Omar and Michael can't be a hundred-percent positive that he didn't, but they're pretty sure.)*

THOMASINA: That isn't funny Thomas!

THOMAS: I'm not trying to be funny. I poisoned you.

MICHAEL: Why would you say something like that?

THOMAS: Because it's true. You're all poisoned.

OMAR: Well I don't feel anything. If I drank poison I would feel it. I'm very sensitive to what goes on in my body.

THOMAS: You're not going to feel anything until *(He checks his watch)* 10:30.

THOMASINA: Thomas, what the hell is wrong with you?

DESMOND: My drink.

MICHAEL: What about it?

DESMOND: It tasted like iodine.

OMAR: That's right! Desmond said his drink tasted like iodine. What did you put in our drinks, Thomas?

THOMAS: Something I found on the internet.

THOMASINA: You looked up how to poison us on the internet?

MICHAEL: Is this your idea of a joke?

THOMAS: Michael, I'm truly sorry, I wasn't expecting you tonight.

DESMOND: I'm not ready!

THOMASINA: Don't be silly, Desmond. None of us is going to die.

MICHAEL: Is this seriously happening right now? Who does this?

OMAR: Are you really going to make me call an ambulance, Thomas? You want to take things that far?

*(Thomas drinks, impassive. Omar takes out his phone and starts dialing.)*

THOMASINA: You stop this right now Thomas! This is the most horrible thing I've ever seen anyone do!

OMAR *(On his phone)*: Hello? Can we please get an ambulance immediately at 99 Washington Avenue? Four people have been poisoned.

*(Thomasina and Michael roll their eyes.)*

We don't know—the person who poisoned us won't tell us what it is. But he says we'll all be dead by . . .

THOMAS: 10:30.

OMAR: 10:30.

Okay, thank you.

She said they'd be here as soon as possible.

THOMAS: Five.

OMAR: What?

THOMAS: Five people have been poisoned. I didn't want to do it by myself.

DESMOND: I'm not ready!

THOMASINA: What the hell is going on?

MICHAEL: This is fucked-up.

DESMOND: My drink tasted like iodine!

THOMASINA: Why would you do this, Thomas?

THOMAS: Because you're all terrible fucking people, except for you Michael.

OMAR: What are you talking about? YOU'RE a terrible fucking person!

DESMOND: I told Charlie that the cocaine he found in my office belonged to Thomas!

THOMASINA: Oh my God . . . Thomas what have I ever done to you?

THOMAS: You're always patronizing me!

THOMASINA: What are you talking about?

THOMAS: You do it constantly! Like the other day when you were talking about how the students at Berkeley have *more access* to their professors than the students at Stanford even though their class sizes are twenty times bigger!

THOMASINA: So? You went to Berkeley and I went to Stanford!

THOMAS: I don't know! You always manage to make everything sound like an insult, like you needed to console me for going to a less prestigious state school with huge class sizes!

THOMASINA: That is such bullshit, Thomas! You're totally projecting!

THOMAS: No I'm not! You do it constantly and it makes me want to fucking strangle you!

MICHAEL: He's making all of this up. This guy is crazy.

THOMASINA: Thomas are you crazy?

THOMAS: I'm not lying. By 10:30 tonight we'll all be dead.

You know, this isn't going the way I thought it would, so I think I'll be heading up to bed.

Thank you all for coming to my party.

Again Michael, I'm very sorry.

Good night.

*(He exits.*
*Pause.*
*He reenters.)*

I'm totally fucking with you guys.

THOMASINA: Thomas!

MICHAEL: Thomas, I must say that I'm inclined to beat the shit out of you.

DESMOND: Do it.

OMAR: You are such an ASSHOLE!

*(Omar attacks Thomas, who doesn't defend himself, and they fall to the ground.*

*Michael pulls Omar off of Thomas. Omar kicks his legs in the air and yells for Michael to put him down. Thomas remains sprawled out on the floor.*

*Michael and Thomasina confer in a corner. Desmond goes to the bar cart and starts making a tequila sunrise.)*

OMAR *(On his phone)*: Hello? I just called from 99 Washington Avenue. Yes. It was a false alarm. Someone was playing a joke.

Thank you. I'm sorry, even though it wasn't my fault.

*(He hangs up and addresses the others.)*

I'm calling a car. Would anyone else like one?

THOMASINA: It would be great if you could get one for Michael and myself.

DESMOND: Yes, please.

THOMAS: WAIT!

OMAR: Hello, could we please get three cars at—

*(Thomas runs and grabs the phone out of Omar's hand.)*

THOMAS: Omar, please wait! Everyone!

I'm sorry. I know you all hate me right now and that I did a really fucked-up, horrible thing, and I'm sorry.

But I am losing my fucking mind. I'm losing it. And if you all leave here tonight then I will definitely kill myself.

OMAR: Fuck you, Thomas! Give me my phone!

DESMOND *(On his phone)*: Hello? Can you please send three cars to—?

THOMAS: PLEASE PLEASE PLEASE PLEASE PLEASE PLEASE PLEASE! DON'T LEAVE ME! DON'T LEAVE ME! DON'T LEAVE ME!

*(He grabs a bottle of scotch off the coffee table and sits cross-legged on the floor downstage, drinking from it.)*

DESMOND *(On his phone)*: Never mind.

MICHAEL: I guess we shouldn't just leave him here like this.

THOMASINA: I've never seen him behave even remotely like this before. I don't know what to do.

DESMOND: When my cousin Edward threatened to kill himself, we had him institutionalized.

THOMASINA: Well, we're not having Thomas locked up so you can put that out of your mind right now Desmond.

OMAR: Thomas, what's going on. Why are you doing this?

THOMASINA: Are you depressed?

THOMAS: I'm lonely. I haven't been in a real relationship for two and a half years.

OMAR: I haven't been in a relationship for longer than that and you don't see me threatening to kill myself!

THOMAS: I'm tired of going to sleep alone and waking up alone. Sometime I need physical contact so badly I think I'll die. You know when you're in bed with someone and they lie right up next to you with their head on your shoulder, and it's like they're a battery and you're their recharger? I need that!

MICHAEL: I know, Thomas. My girlfriend Shannon is horrible to me, but I can't break up with her because then we wouldn't be able to get into that battery recharge position.

THOMAS: And I'm tired of just having sex with people. It would be one thing if they just materialized in my bed and then disappeared right after I came, but it's so much effort to go out and buy drinks and make conversation and work out. I'm getting too old for this! I'm thirty, goddammit!

THOMASINA: Thirty's not that old, Thomas. I'm almost twenty-six.

THOMAS: And I'm sick of my job! I hate going there every day. I want to be able to earn a living by sitting at home doing whatever I want!

THOMASINA: Thomas I'm sure we all feel that way.

DESMOND: I like my job.

THOMAS: Also, sometimes when I'm talking to someone, I realize that I've said something I shouldn't have said. And that makes me feel bad. And sometimes I feel bad for a long time after I've said the bad thing. And sometimes I curse myself in my mind or even out loud.

OMAR: Thomas, I feel like you're trying to copy me.

THOMAS: What are you talking about, Omar?

OMAR: You're trying to copy me!

THOMAS: I'm not trying to copy you, Omar! But you don't have to worry about it because after you leave tonight I'll be dead.

MICHAEL: I'm not leaving then.

THOMASINA: Well I have to leave. Thomas, I have to say I'm really ticked-off at you.

OMAR: I'm ticked-off, too!

THOMAS: I AM ALL ALONE!

*(Thomas stands up and chugs from the bottle.)*

MICHAEL *(To Thomasina)*: Didn't you say Thomas was your most social and happy friend?

THOMASINA: He was!

OMAR: He's definitely my most social and happy friend!

THOMASINA: So what do we do?

MICHAEL: Thomas, I'm going to make some phone calls. We're going to get some help for you, okay?

THOMAS: Okay.

*(Michael exits.*
*Thomas becomes very pathetic.)*

I'm going to the nuthouse!

DESMOND: Shut up, Thomas.

THOMAS: Does anyone want to play Library?

OMAR: We should just let you kill yourself.

THOMAS: Omar, I'm sorry.

*(Omar walks away, Thomas chases him.)*

Omar!

Thomasina, do you want to play Library?

THOMASINA: I'm not really in the mood, Thomas.

OMAR: Desmond said Library is really boring.

THOMASINA: It's actually really fun.

THOMAS: So let's play! Desmond?

*(Desmond doesn't respond.)*

Desmond, I forgive you for what you did to me today. Thanks to you I'll probably get fired. Now we're even, okay?

Thomasina, will you at least explain the rules?

Please?

THOMASINA: Fine, Thomas.

*(Unenthusiastically)* The way you play Library is: someone picks a book, shows us the cover, and tells us the author's name and what kind of book it is—like a biography, a novel, etcetera. Then we each have to make up a sentence that sounds like it would be in that book and write it down. And then we vote on which one is the actual sentence from the book.

DESMOND: You make it sound fun.

THOMAS: I'm going to go get some paper and pens. Omar, why don't you pick a book. I know you'll pick a good one.

*(Thomas exits.*
*Omar contemplates the books.)*

OMAR: I can't believe I'm doing this.

*(Thomas reenters, passing out paper and pens.)*

THOMAS: What did you find, Omar?
OMAR: *Sexual Anorexia: Overcoming Sexual Self-Hatred.*
THOMAS: Ooh!
OMAR: It's a self-help book by Patrick Carnes and Joseph Moriarity. You have to guess the first sentence of this book.

*(Everyone writes.*
*Omar collects everyone's slips of paper, snatching Thomas's paper out of his hand.*
*Omar reads aloud:)*

"There is no reason to be ashamed of your penis and/or vaglna."

*(Thomas shakes with silent laughter. That one was his. Everyone glares at him disgustedly.)*

"They suffer silently, consumed by a dread of sexual pleasure and filled with fear and sexual self-doubt."
THOMAS *(Pointing)*: Ooh, that's the one!

*(Everyone glares at him.)*

OMAR: "Sexual anorexia is a disease."

*(Everyone looks at Desmond. That one is his for sure.)*

"People suffering from sexual anorexia tend to avoid sex."
THOMAS: You guys weren't even trying!

Okay, that was terrible. We're not even gonna vote on that one. That was a warm-up. Let's do another one, a good one this time.

I'll pick.

*(Michael reenters.)*

MICHAEL: An ambulance should be arriving within the next hour. Thomas, they'll be taking you to the hospital for twenty-four-hour observation.

THOMAS *(Crawling on the floor, looking in the coffee table/book shelf for a book)*: Great.

MICHAEL: What the hell are you guys doing? Are you playing Library?!

THOMAS: I found one!

MICHAEL: SERIOUSLY?

THOMAS: This is a nonfiction book called *Black Magic* by Yvonne Patricia Chireau. There's a chapter in this book called "Negro Superstitions" which is made up of a list of black superstitions. You guys have to come up with the first superstition in the list. Your sentence should begin, "The Negro believes."

Omar, you're not going to blog about this, are you?

*(Omar gives him a disgusted look.*
*Everyone writes.)*

THOMASINA: Oh, I'm going to hell.

*(Everyone writes.)*

THOMAS: Is everyone done?

THOMASINA: I'm so going to hell for this.

*(Thomas reads everyone's slips of paper.)*

THOMAS: "The Negro believes that cod liver oil cures cancer."
"The Negro believes."

THOMASINA: Yes?

THOMAS: That's all it says, is "The Negro believes."
Hm.

*(Thomas looks suspiciously at Omar.)*

"The Negro believes that a pumpkin in an advanced stage of ripeness has healing properties."
    "The Negro believes that a stutterer may be cured by rubbing him up and down with a raw beef tongue."

*(Thomasina looks at Michael. That one was his. He crosses his arms and shrugs.)*

*(Bursting out laughing)* "The Negro believes that a Negro's hands and feet are white because the moon done touched 'em in Africa!"

*(Thomasina cracks up. That one was hers. Michael starts laughing as well. Thomasina looks at Desmond, laughing, and he laughs loudly in response.)*

OMAR: I'm sorry. I'm sorry, but I have to say that I'm really uncomfortable with all of this.
    I just don't think we'd be doing this if there were a black person in the room.

*(Pause.)*

DESMOND: I guess that would depend on what kind of black person it was.

*(Blackout.)*

END OF PLAY

LEAR

In memory of James M. Lee,
great thinker, non-complainer,
and loving father

*Lear* premiered in January 2010 at Soho Rep in New York City. It was commissioned and co-produced by Soho Rep (Sarah Benson, Artistic Director; Tania Camargo, Executive Director; Rob Marcato, Producer) and Young Jean Lee's Theater Company (Young Jean Lee, Artistic Director; Caleb Hammons, Producing Director). It was written and directed by Young Jean Lee. It was produced by Caleb Hammons. The choreography and stage movement were by Dean Moss, the set design was by David Evans Morris, the lighting design was by Raquel Davis, the costume design was by Roxana Ramseur, the sound design was by Matthew Tierney; the dramaturg was Mike Farry, the associate director was Lee Sunday Evans and the production stage manager was Anthony Cerrato. It was performed by:

| | |
|---|---|
| EDGAR, PAUL, GORDON | Paul Lazar |
| REGAN, APRIL, SUSAN | April Matthis |
| GONERIL, OKWUI, MARIA | Okwui Okpokwasili |
| EDMUND, PETE, BIG BIRD | Pete Simpson |
| CORDELIA, AMELIA, OLIVIA | Amelia Workman |

The following synopsis is handed out to the audience along with their programs:

"A Partial and Approximately Accurate Synopsis of Shakespeare's *King Lear*"

King Lear was an old man who ruled England for many years. He had three grown daughters named Goneril, Regan and Cordelia. One day, Lear decided to retire from the burdens of ruling. He intended to divide his kingdom among all of his daughters, until he began to suspect that his youngest daughter Cordelia did not love him. Enraged, he disinherited her and sentenced her to banishment. At the time, two kings, France and Burgundy, were in Lear's court vying for Cordelia's hand. Lear tried to humiliate his daughter by presenting her to them, banished and without a dowry. France chose to marry her anyway and took her to France. In her absence, Regan and Goneril shared their father's lands between them. Soon they fell out with Lear. They barred him from his former castles, leaving him out in a storm, where he began to go mad.

Lear's closest advisor was another old man named Gloucester. Gloucester had two sons, Edgar and Edmund (a bastard). Gloucester tried to aid the old king behind Goneril and Regan's backs, but was exposed by Edmund. Goneril and Regan seized Gloucester, blinded him (Regan did the actual blinding), and sent him into the storm to join their father.

Our show begins roughly at this point in the story. Nothing else that happens in Shakespeare's text is necessarily relevant to what you are about to see.

Note on Casting

Goneril, Regan and Cordelia should be played by women of color.

*There is a Gothic-arched proscenium with ornate bas-relief detail: rosettes, trefoils, and diamond latticework in golds and copper with scarlet accents and hints of lapis lazuli. There is also an elaborately patterned red-and-gold curtain with heavy gold fringe.*

*An ominous, pulsating rumbling sound plays continuously as the audience enters.*

*The curtain rises on Goneril and Regan in a throne room, doing a stately, measured Elizabethan court dance to consort music ("Mistresse Nichols Almand" by John Dowland). They smile with real pleasure as they dance.*

*The side walls of the throne room consist of mahogany panels in the shape of columns, between which are recessed panels filled with red damask. There are twin-armed candelabra sconces mounted on each column, backed by gold sun-shaped mirrors. Above the panels are diamond-pane windows made of clear, red, and yellow leaded glass. There are two benches of dark paneled wood and red upholstery downstage left and right, and two entrances, midstage left and right, through Gothic archways.*

*A huge gilded throne, intricately carved with winged-lion armrests and upholstered in tufted red velvet, sits on a large, two-tiered dais upstage center. The throne is flanked by two smaller, but equally baroque, red-and-gold armchairs. Red Persian rugs cover the floor and dais.*

*There is an arched back wall covered in Gothic tracery with ornate medallions at the intersections, all in gold woodwork on a red field covered with gold-leaf sunbursts. The tracery radiates out around the throne like a peacock or explosion.*

*Goneril and Regan wear sumptuous Elizabethan gowns with full skirts—Goneril in royal purple, Regan in emerald. The dresses are made of velvet, satin, and metallic jacquards with standing white lace collars, open bustlines, and gold trimmings and beltings. The women wear necklaces, pendants, rings, and bracelets, as well as elaborate wigs with bejeweled hair ornaments.*

*Edgar and Edmund enter and join in the dance, creating more intricate patterns. Everyone smiles and dances with real pleasure.*

*The men wear Elizabethan doublets and pumpkin breeches made from rich black fabrics with metallic accents in the cloth and trimmings—gold for Edgar and silver for Edmund. They have stiffly tailored ruffs and lace cuffs, elaborate chains-of-office, necklaces, rings, and lavishly trimmed capes. Ornate swords carried in scabbards hang from their belts. Edgar wears a fake mustache and goatee that he will later remove.*

*The dance ends with all four dancers holding hands with their bodies facing outward, skipping in a circle. As the music ends, they break the circle to assume their positions for the following scene. Regan sits on the stage-right bench, Goneril sits on the stage-left bench, Edgar sits on the dais upstage left, and Edmund stands upstage right.*

*Blackout with lit candles and loud, ominous rumbling.*

*Lights up. Faint consort music ("Semper Dowland semper dolens" by John Dowland) plays.*

*Goneril reads a book, Regan does needlepoint, and Edgar polishes his sword. Edmund is deep in tortured thought.*

*Pause.*

*Edmund makes a noise of anguish. Everyone ignores him.*

*Pause.*

*Edmund makes a louder noise of anguish and is once again ignored.*

EDGAR: Edmund and I just enjoyed the most wonderful meal.
REGAN: What did you have?
EDGAR: Six different roasted meats and fowls, new potatoes, spring
    sausage, onion soup, and gooseberry tart with country cream.
GONERIL: Lovely.
EDGAR: The soup was covered by nearly an *inch* of baked cheese.

GONERIL: Goodness, Edgar. How did you—
EDMUND: I'm a bad person!

*(Pause.)*

EDGAR: Why.
EDMUND: I only care about myself.
REGAN: Everyone is selfish.
EDMUND: I betrayed my father. He's out in the storm with his eyes gouged out!
EDGAR: Our father was a traitor!

*(Pause.)*

EDMUND: Plus, everyone is starting to look fat to me.
EDGAR: What do you mean?
EDMUND: Everyone looks fat. Regan looks fat, you look fat. Unless someone is completely skeletal with no muscle or anything, I think they look fat.
GONERIL: That's really evil.
EDMUND: I know!
REGAN: But you're not a bad person.
EDMUND: Then who is?
REGAN: Torturers working in a torture center.
EDMUND: But what would I do if I was in that position, I'm not . . . I want to win, to fit the pattern . . . would I have taken babies by their legs and smashed them against trees? I don't know! If the torture center is getting too full and your superiors tell you to kill people off in a less expensive way . . . people always manage to justify doing horrible things.
EDGAR: What is wrong with you today, Edmund?
EDMUND: Nothing.

*(Pause.)*

I suck!
EDGAR: But you have the raw material to become something great. If only you could see your own value as I do, buried beneath your excess weight.

EDMUND: Everything sucks!

REGAN: The world is full of things, and you just fight them off. Because what are you going to do? Nothing. So you have to accept them.

EDMUND: But the pain.

EDGAR: I have to say that I believe the true answer lies in Buddhism.

REGAN: Buddhism is great.

GONERIL: I really like Buddhism, and all the psychology that comes out of that, with that influence.

EDMUND: What do you mean by Buddhism?

EDGAR: You know, like with . . . like you just accept everything. If something bad happens then you just accept it.

REGAN: When a thought comes into your head you just label it "thinking" and it helps.

GONERIL: And also, another thing about Buddhism is that . . . I don't know, I just like it.

*(Pause.)*

EDMUND: I'm losing my hair.

REGAN: How awful.

GONERIL: How can people stand to be bald.

REGAN: I don't know. I think most people think they look pretty good. I don't think they would leave the house otherwise.

EDGAR: I think most people have that body and face dysmorphia, you know, only in the opposite direction. Like, they think they look better than they do.

REGAN: People's bodies are just tragic.

EDGAR: Maybe some day modern technology will be able to cure that, you know?

GONERIL: Yeah, how do old people, how can they even bear to touch each other?

EDGAR: Some day modern technology is going to advance to the point where that really helps us out a lot.

GONERIL: Do you ever play that game where you're . . . it's called "Who Won?" and you're looking at couples on the street and you ask yourself, "Who won?"

EDGAR: That game doesn't work unless you know what the guy does for a living.

REGAN: People are such . . . and people have such mean personalities.

EDGAR: Yeah someone who's . . . Oh and you know what pisses me off?

EDMUND: What?

EDGAR: Why can't women be more feminine!

EDMUND: Oh I know!

EDGAR: Yeah it's like they go around wearing frumpy underwear and . . . how do they expect anyone to stay attracted to them?

EDMUND: You know what I love?

EDGAR: What.

EDMUND: Garter belts.

EDGAR: Holy shit that is like the hottest thing ever. But women never do that shit, it's like . . . why can't the women I'm with be more feminine.

GONERIL: You know what's annoying to me?

REGAN: What.

GONERIL: How *fat* guys get.

EDMUND: Women get fat too!

REGAN: It's like a prerequisite for all of you to get a gut.

GONERIL: It makes you look pregnant, how disgusting.

REGAN: Also, do you know how pathetic your careers look to us? We pretend to admire you but actually a lot of times we feel sorry for you.

EDGAR: Well, men act devoted because they know you expect it, when actually they don't think you're *that* hot and they get obsessed with other women all the time.

EDMUND: And we tell our friends about it, too.

*(Blackout with loud rumbling.*
   *Edgar and Edmund exit.*
   *Lights up. Goneril is on the stage-left bench with Regan standing near her. Soft rumbling.)*

GONERIL: I'm a bad person.

REGAN: I'm the one who did it.

GONERIL: That's true.

REGAN: I'm the one who did the bad thing to the old man with the gouging of the eyes and so forth, letting him bleed into the snow.

GONERIL: There was no snow.

REGAN: There can be snow if I say so.

GONERIL: Okay.

REGAN: I say there was a *lot* of snow and that his eyes bled rings into the ground, burrowing down.

GONERIL: Stop it, Regan.

REGAN: I can see our father.

GONERIL: Don't say that.

REGAN: I can see him in the storm, bleeding rings into the ground.

GONERIL: That's Edgar and Edmund's father.

REGAN: Our father is out there too.

GONERIL: Shut up.

REGAN: I can see the coffin coming.
    Funerals are good.

GONERIL: Sometimes I feel sad at them but other times I feel like, look at all the fashion.

REGAN: I can see his eyes bleeding rings into the ground.

GONERIL: That's not our father. That's the other one.

REGAN: I know, but we did it.

GONERIL: You did it.

REGAN: You would have done it.

GONERIL: No I wouldn't. That's not my style.

REGAN: All right.

GONERIL: It's your style, there's no shame in that.
    Like Satan.

REGAN: Satan was an asshole because he was afraid, not because he was selfish. Those are mutually exclusive things.

*(All sound cuts out. Lights out except for lit candles and a spotlight on Goneril, standing.)*

GONERIL: I am a woman and my name is Goneril. And oh, how I long to be good to you. That is all I wish is to be good to the people around me, to make them feel whole and important so that they will dance to my bidding and bend to my will. This is how I operate. Not by cruelty and power, but by passivity and sickness. I am sick right now. My poor father is abandoned and in pain and I feel his suffering as if it were my own. I shed tears upon his poor bald head, but what am I to do? My needs are essential. If I want to kick you to the curb, that is because my foot is possessed by the desire of kicking. I have no control over myself. I am a poor weak-willed woman with no strength who wishes nothing more than to please you and make you feel good about yourself. I am a lavish tipper. I will love you as you are serving me. I will make endless conversation with you and express interest in your work and home life and feel over-whelming pity for the hardship of your circumstances as you angle for a larger tip, and I will give you the tip of a lifetime. And you will experience five seconds of pleasure before the grinding everyday misery of your life gives way to the grind-ing everyday misery of heat and cold and intemperate climes. And I will step into the sweltering ballroom in my finery and dance with a skill acquired after years of fighting my natural instincts to be lumbering and grotesque. I am a champion over everything. And this is a power that only women know. The power in weakness, the power in ugliness and clumsiness and the hiding of our true natures in deception, but actually that's not true at all. You can read everything on our faces. You don't need me to tell you a word.

*(Blackout with loud rumbling.*

*Lights up. Goneril is on the stage-left bench and Regan is on the stage-right bench. Soft rumbling.)*

Something is different with Cordelia's teeth.
REGAN: Her . . . she looks like she's been sharpening.
GONERIL: And she's come back with all the French fashions.
REGAN: She looks better than ever I have to say, although . . .
GONERIL: She's shiny, somehow.
REGAN: Maybe she just needs to blot.
GONERIL: There is something . . . she seems confident.
REGAN: She looks like an Angel of Death.

*(Sound of footsteps echoing down the hall.*

*Cordelia enters, gorgeously arrayed. Faint lute music ["My Ladie Riches Galyerd" by John Dowland] plays over soft rumbling.*

*Cordelia wears an opulent, cleavage-baring sapphire gown fea-turing an excess of jewels, beading, and red bows on her bodice and skirt. Her wig is taller and more ornamented than her sisters', with blue and cream feathers rising out of the top.*

*Cordelia smiles. There is something inexplicably terrifying about her.)*

GONERIL: Hi Cordelia, what have you been doing all day?
CORDELIA: Nothing.
REGAN: It's nice to have you back home.
CORDELIA: I'm happy about it.
GONERIL: How was France?
CORDELIA: Lovely, thank you.
REGAN: And how is France your husband?
CORDELIA: He is well.
GONERIL: Did you have some work done on your teeth?
CORDELIA: No.
GONERIL: They look lovely. Very sharp.
CORDELIA: Thank you.

*(Cordelia takes a step toward Goneril, who shrinks away.)*

REGAN: So what is France like?
CORDELIA: Lots of blue. Lots of gray. Massive clocks embedded in the stone, with the clouds drifting by. Lovely.
GONERIL: Lovely.
REGAN: We were so sorry about how you left.
CORDELIA: I'm sure you were.
GONERIL: We really were.
REGAN: Dad was wrong to throw you out.
CORDELIA: I accept that you thought you were sorry. I have learned acceptance.
GONERIL: How did you cope?
CORDELIA: Do you really want to know?
REGAN: Yes.

*(The music fades out. The lights brighten around Cordelia.)*

CORDELIA: I started to drink.
GONERIL: Goodness.
CORDELIA: I drank and forced myself upon animals.

REGAN: Heavens.

CORDELIA: I tried to molest my husband with a toothbrush.

GONERIL: Really?

CORDELIA: And then the glorious reformation.

Now I don't drink a drop.

GONERIL: Wonderful!

REGAN: Congratulations to you, Cordelia.

*(The music resumes. The lights go back to normal.)*

CORDELIA: I have forgiven the king our father.

GONERIL: Good for you, dear sister!

CORDELIA: Speaking of which, where is the old bastard?

REGAN: Well.

GONERIL: That's the thing.

CORDELIA: What's the thing? I wish to shower him with scalding flames of love.

REGAN: He's not here.

CORDELIA: Not here? Where is he?

GONERIL: In the storm.

CORDELIA: Why?

REGAN: We kicked him out.

CORDELIA: You kicked him out?

GONERIL: Yes.

CORDELIA: But why?

REGAN: He wanted to go.

CORDELIA *(Perturbed)*: Why then he must be dead.

*(Goneril looks upset.)*

REGAN: Cordelia, how did you survive your banishment?

CORDELIA: I told myself that I was happy. I said it over and over until it became true. And now I am the happiest girl alive.

*(Cordelia bares her teeth.)*

REGAN: Lovely.

CORDELIA: I told the world to be what it was, come what may, and I would transform shit into sugar blossoms.

REGAN: Wow.

CORDELIA: And I chose to love every greedy pustule of a human on this earth. That was all there really was to it.

*(Goneril stands suddenly. The music cuts out, leaving only the soft rumbling.)*

GONERIL: Dad might still be alive!

*(She sits back down.)*

I want to know what he's doing.

REGAN: He's in the rain, he's wet. He's cursing our cunts.

GONERIL: He's all alone.

REGAN: Your guilt will protect you.

GONERIL: He's suffering so much.

CORDELIA: That's life.

GONERIL: Then it'll happen to us.

REGAN: In one form or another.

GONERIL: Horrible.

CORDELIA: You have to embrace it.

GONERIL: I can't.

CORDELIA: Then you'll suffer more.

GONERIL: I can feel it happening.

REGAN: You're in your prime.

GONERIL: And then downhill.

CORDELIA: It's already happening.

GONERIL: I'm going to feel what he feels.

REGAN: Everyone dies.

GONERIL: Then why live. What is there.

REGAN: Sometimes the weather has sun to warm and shade to cover and breeze to cool. And sometimes there are deer and fat possums and sometimes, but not usually, there is cold chicken and ginger beer and one time, one time there was a pie.

CORDELIA: What kind of pie?

REGAN: Mince pie.

CORDELIA: Holy moly.

REGAN: Please be happy in it. Rejoice in every little detail. The bits of music you can pick out from the distance, the boringness of boring things.

CORDELIA: I am grateful for the gray street, the white dome, the gold statue against a blue sky.

*(All sound cuts out. Lights out except for lit candles and a spotlight on Regan.)*

REGAN: I wake up in the morning and I am alive. My eyes are open and I can see. You should write down a list of things that are important to you and work toward those things, but what if everything fills your gorge like a goose with the tubing and the grain forced down the throat and into the stomach to fatten the liver with delights for those who know what they want. They want that delectation on crusty bread with a simple wine and company, except for the man dining alone, the man in the soft sweater and tasteful jacket who is eating soup and talking animatedly to himself. The gray-haired man with the kindly face, enjoying crammed liver and witty conversation all alone. Some things are unspeakable. What does his heart look like. If I held him, he would struggle like a puppy with the crushed paw, mammal softness squeezed to death. I would comfort you, old man. Hold still and be silent. This is my love that I am offering to you as something acceptable in the world. Please don't cry out as I attempt to love you. I apologize for interrupting your meal but I can't bear the pleasure in your laugh and must put out the light in your smiling face. It is not permissible for you to enjoy yourself in this way. Hold your head still as I remove first one and then the other, gently with my tongue, prodding your sockets the light to remove, to cease what must be ceased for the moment and not a second too late. I have decided that misery is unacceptable. We are two of a kind, only I suffer the pains that you avoid through being undesirable. Lie down and be still and await the fate that is awaiting you.

*(Back to regular light, soft rumbling.)*

*(To Goneril)* When is the last time you slept?

GONERIL: When is the last time *you* slept?

*(Edgar and Edmund enter with a loud rumble. They bow. The loud rumble fades to soft rumbling.)*

CORDELIA: Hello Edgar and Edmund.

EDMUND: Hello.

EDGAR: Edmund and I were just out for a walk. Actually we were not out for a walk, we were talking in a dank, unlit closet because we were discussing men's affairs.

CORDELIA: All right.

REGAN: I remember Edgar in his short pants.

EDGAR: I was a little soldier. And Edmund was my executive officer.

CORDELIA *(To Edmund)*: Your mother would curl your hair.

EDMUND: My hair was naturally curly.

CORDELIA: I saw her put your hair up in papers myself.

EDMUND: I fought against her. I kicked her in the crotch.

CORDELIA: No, that happened when she said you were too old for curling papers.

GONERIL: There were so many things to be upset about that we didn't notice.

REGAN: We all went to the seaside.

EDGAR: We climbed over the railings and dropped in the water.

CORDELIA: The air smelled like sugar.

GONERIL: There were bright colors and freaks of nature and oh my heart, my heart my heart my heart.

REGAN: What about it?

GONERIL: It makes my heart. There are things trying to intrude.

*(Goneril runs out.)*

EDMUND: What's wrong with Goneril?

EDGAR: Her face has aged so much. She used to be the hottest one out of all of you.

REGAN: Edgar.

EDGAR: Yes?

REGAN: I don't want to be friends with you anymore.

EDGAR: Why?

REGAN: You're always saying shitty things.

*(Edgar bows before Regan.)*

EDGAR: I'm very sorry if I offended you Regan! That was not my intention.

REGAN: I don't care about your intentions.

EDGAR: Are you serious?

REGAN: When something hurts me, I cut it out.

*(Regan exits.)*

EDGAR: At the rate she's going, pretty soon there won't be anyone left.

*(Blackout with lit candles and loud rumbling.*

*Lights up. Cordelia is on the stage-right bench with Edmund standing near her. Faint lute music ["Orlando Sleepeth" by John Dowland] plays over soft rumbling.)*

EDMUND: Cordelia I love you.

CORDELIA: What kind.

EDMUND: Romantic.

CORDELIA: I only want the spiritual kind that would love me the same with limbs or as a stump.

EDMUND: There is no such love.

CORDELIA: I have felt such a love. That is the love I feel for you in this moment.

EDMUND: And no more, Cordelia?

CORDELIA: No.

EDMUND: Why not?

CORDELIA: You would never survive it. Why don't you run away.

EDMUND: I will never run away! Intensity is my master and it shall direct me in the ways in which I wish to be directed, and the rain shall fall and pierce my tongue as I drip blood upon the land. I shall be whole and free and my spirits will soar at my bidding, my legs will skip to my bidding, my mouth shall laugh at my bidding, and the rain will fall and fall upon my head and lightning will strike my eyes and I shall suffocate inside mine own face! This is what the Lord has taught me and this is the lesson I shall take to my grave.

CORDELIA: Okay, I will have you.

EDMUND: Really?

CORDELIA: No I'm just kidding.

EDMUND: That's not fair!

I have unique qualities.

CORDELIA: Such as?

EDMUND: My sense of perspective.

CORDELIA: Gross.

EDMUND: I'm not as safe as I seem.

CORDELIA: How so?

EDMUND: First of all, my true love is Goneril.

CORDELIA: Really?

EDMUND: But she will not have me.

CORDELIA: Huh.

EDMUND: I would cherish you for as long as we dwelt in the same house as her.

CORDELIA: It's a tempting offer.

EDMUND: Cordelia, I vow and swear that I will always give you something to hope for.

Have you always worn your hair like that?

CORDELIA: I think so. Why?

EDMUND: It looks different.

CORDELIA: In a bad way?

*(Pause.)*

EDMUND: No.

CORDELIA: You must hate me.

EDMUND: Yes, but it's not personal. I only hate you insofar as your imperfections contrast with her glories.

CORDELIA: So much shall your suffering increase once I turn the tables.

EDMUND: That suffering is sweeter to me than any cunt.

CORDELIA: My cunt shall—

EDMUND: Enough of this, Cordelia! I love you and only you.

You love me too.

CORDELIA: I suppose.

EDMUND: Say it, Cordelia, or I shall pluck out my manhood before your very eyes!

CORDELIA: I love you and only you. I love you so much that I don't even feel it as love.

EDMUND: Why in Heaven's name will you not be mine?

CORDELIA: I am Cordelia and I am good and there are fine candy-spun things sweetening my dreams. I will cry into your ear and give you something to be sorry about. I will show how many pastries it takes to suffocate a baby calf. And your diaphragm will be safe from me, I will not remove it in soft handfuls, I will not extract your tongue with my teeth. Soon you will understand the sweetness of crying, of ears and sorriness and pastries and calves and diaphragms and tongues, each one as soothing as the last, and this is none of this as damning as it sounds, you will enjoy it. You dread and fear it because you know not what it is, but once you feel the softness you will sing through your gags and stuffings and that disposable face of yours will be ours, because you were made to be ours, you were made for health and kindness. Because what is there to love other than healing, other than breath and strength and heart and life and feedings? There will be many more feedings than this in your future, I assure you. I will love your face and ears and eyes and voice until you are crying in fear and desolation. I guarantee that you will be weeping, but for what? Why not rejoice? I will wipe your bloody rings and make them full of pastry. You will be stuffed until there is nothing left of you but crashing waves and bloody bowls and mucous overflowing an empty stomach.

*(Cordelia leans in to kiss Edmund, who recoils and turns away. The music ends.*
*Blackout with loud rumbling.*
*All sound cuts out. A spotlight on Edgar standing on the dais.)*

EDGAR: What is it like to be a singer. You stand up there and the charisma is all over you and your voice is soaring and everyone is blown away. I remember when I was in school there was one day when I showed up and half the class was missing from the flu. All the athletes were gone, the teacher was out sick, and the substitute had gone to the wrong place so we were sitting there together, all the girls and us nerdy boys, and I suddenly became the leader. I have no idea how it happened. I organized everyone into groups and gave them these fun projects, and everyone was excited and listening to me and I was going around praising people's work. It was great. And the next time I went to school I thought maybe something would be changed toward me, but the popular kids were back and everyone had forgotten it ever happened. In my whole life, from beginning to end, that was my one day of glory. What must it be like for people who have every day like that.

The funny thing is I actually have a good singing voice. It's not consistent and I have a small vocal range, but if something were exactly in my range and I practiced it, I think I could maybe move people.

*(Back to regular light, soft rumbling. Edgar is on the dais and Edmund is on the stage-left bench.)*

EDMUND: I want revenge.

EDGAR: For what?

EDMUND: What they did to Dad.

EDGAR: What are you talking about? You're the one who gave him away.

EDMUND: You wanted it too.

EDGAR: I accepted it.

*(Pause.)*

EDMUND: Want to go eat?

EDGAR: No thanks.

EDMUND: Wow, really?

EDGAR: I can't swallow.

EDMUND: When's the last time you slept?

EDGAR: I don't remember.

EDMUND: Hey, look at this.

*(Edmund demonstrates a sword thrust.)*

EDGAR: Don't you even want to know what happened when I went out looking for him?

EDMUND: No.

EDGAR: Why not?

EDMUND: You're going to blame me.

EDGAR: I promised you a million times I wouldn't.

EDMUND: Even if you don't blame me with your mouth, you'll blame me with your face.

EDGAR: I won't!

EDMUND: Fine. What happened.

EDGAR: I was in the storm looking for Dad, and at first I had negative thoughts but I just kept praying and soul-searching until I became almost euphoric with peace.

EDMUND: You're blaming me with your eyes!

EDGAR: The rain was beating on me and lightning was toppling the trees, but I am a fundamentally kind person, somehow, although actually I am not. I kick beggars. I do that one cruel thing. I wear extremely expensive and heavy boots and I kick beggars every chance I get. I kick them as hard as I can.

No just kidding. I've never kicked a beggar in my life and my boots are neither heavy nor expensive because I am an impecunious skinflint.

EDMUND: What are you talking about?

EDGAR: If I hadn't gone out into that stupid storm then I would . . . I was out there for like a week searching. I couldn't have stayed less with any decency. I wasted all that time but it wasn't a waste because I found Dad. He wanted a cliff so he could kill himself but I got him to jump on flat ground and fall on his face and he learned a lesson and I came back here. No, he died first and then I came back here. He died.

EDMUND: He died?

EDGAR: Yes I told him I am Edgar and his heart broke and he died.

EDMUND: Why'd you do that?

EDGAR: I wanted him to recognize me.

If I hadn't gone out into that stupid storm I'd have so much time right now.

EDMUND: Our father is dead.

EDGAR: Nobody knows what I go through! They say, "Edgar is so reliable." No they don't even say I'm reliable, they just expect me to show up and do the right thing every time without any credit except for when I fuck up and then I'm not reliable. "Edgar must go to the ball!" "Edgar must be in the storm!" "Edgar must know the meaning of life!" I'm sick of it!

EDMUND: Nobody made you do anything!
  What's wrong with you?
EDGAR: Nothing.
EDMUND: Where did you go?
EDGAR: I was in the storm, on a tramp steamer, smoking corncob
  pipes, etcetera. What do you care where I was?
EDMUND: You never found our father.
EDGAR: Yes I did.
EDMUND: Is he dead or isn't he?
EDGAR: What did I say, Bastard.
EDMUND: Don't call me Bastard.
EDGAR: Oh I'm not calling you Bastard. I'm talking to that wall over
  there. I named that wall Bastard. Hey, Bastard, you're looking
  pretty stupid today.
EDMUND: You're looking right at me!
EDGAR: No I'm not, I'm looking at the wall. Hey, Bastard, why don't
  you come lay your balls on my face?
EDMUND: What?
EDGAR *(Moving toward Edmund)*: Come inside my womb, boy!
EDMUND: You don't have a womb!
EDGAR: The man is the ultimate womb of the universe! I've got
  wombs like you've never seen.
EDMUND: Get away from me!
EDGAR: Come with your tits into my face!

*(Edgar nuzzles imaginary breasts on Edmund, who pushes him away.)*

EDMUND: Don't do this, Edgar!
  Come with YOUR tits into MY face!

*(Edmund lunges for Edgar's chest and tries to lick his nipple.
Edgar jerks away, causing Edmund to fall to the floor.)*

EDGAR: Stop it, Edmund!

*(Edmund lunges with his head toward Edgar's crotch and Edgar runs
away.)*

EDMUND *(On his knees)*: Come with your dingle-dongle right into
  my face and fill me up like an éclair from France!

*(Edmund gets up and Edgar eyes him warily. Edmund lunges toward Edgar with his tongue out, as if trying to make out with him. Edgar grabs Edmund by the throat and they grapple.)*

EDGAR: I would kill you in an instant if it were a choice between your life and my looks! You do not believe this is true but it is absolutely true!

*(They grapple, switching positions so that Edmund has Edgar by the throat.)*

EDMUND: Were the choice between your life and a panful of acid thrown into my face, I would choose the pan of acid! Because one's face is a horrible thing!

*(Blackout.*
   *In the dark, a loud, throbbing rumble shakes the risers. Light comes up slowly, isolating the throne, as Regan and Cordelia enter slowly in silhouette, stage left and stage right, respectively. They walk toward each other, stop, turn upstage, walk up the dais, and sit in the chairs on either side of the throne, Regan stage left and Cordelia stage right, slowly and in unison. They pause for a moment in profile, looking at each other.*
   *As they turn their heads to face front, the lights come up fully. The loud throbbing cuts abruptly to a soft rumble.)*

REGAN: My ceiling is leaking.
CORDELIA: There are always horrible things. I have bedbugs.
REGAN: I hear it dripping all night.
CORDELIA: I have bedbugs! I would chop off my pinkie finger without hesitation if it would guarantee that I would never have to see another bedbug again.
REGAN: I don't know anything about bedbugs and I don't want to know! I'll start feeling like I have them.
CORDELIA: They are the worst.
REGAN: Oh no I have bedbugs.
CORDELIA: You do not!
REGAN: I have bedbugs I have bedbugs!

*(Regan starts giggling weirdly.)*

CORDELIA: It's an insult to tell a person who has actual bedbugs that you have imaginary ones!

*(Edmund bursts in with his sword out.*
*Throughout Edmund's following speech, Regan visibly attempts to suppress hysterical laughter.)*

EDMUND *(Brandishing his sword at Cordelia and Regan)*: I know where you are vulnerable and I will pierce you in your eye sockets for all of the indignities of being a man despite my sword, despite my power! I must not be petted like a cow! I must be fondled in sickness and then cast away in disgust! But I know things that have been settled for generations and I have my rights and my means and I am a man!

*(Regan bursts out laughing.)*

You must respect my automations!

*(Edmund runs out, humiliated, as Regan laughs hysterically.*
*Regan laughs uncontrollably. Cordelia is disturbed.)*

CORDELIA: When's the last time you ate?
REGAN: This morning.
CORDELIA: What did you eat?
REGAN: Some dates.
CORDELIA: You look terrible.
REGAN: I feel terrible.
CORDELIA: Why?
REGAN: Bad dreams.
CORDELIA: About what?
REGAN: About a filthy-faced woman who said that there'd been a rape. "A rape?" I asked. "When?" And she said, "A few minutes ago. Run!" And just as she said the word "run" another woman wearing a brown wig grabbed me and held me fast with weak fingers. She spoke of the things she would do to me, meditating on the pleasures. As she spoke, her wig would shift and

I could see her real hair underneath, which was short and gray and caked with dandruff. She mentioned that there was a dump out back. "It would be a good place to serve you," she said. I knew my body would feel every imaginable horror. I stabbed a sharpened pencil into her hand, and there it stuck. She noticed it not. I said, "I stabbed a pencil into your hand," and she said, "You did, did you? Well, I haven't slept in three days and can't feel a thing." I screamed and struggled, and then woke up. I felt the relief that comes from finding your body safe in bed. And then I remembered that he is in the storm. It is happening to him. He is my father. It is happening to him and it will happen to me. Nothing can stop it.

CORDELIA: You're going to be just fine.

REGAN: Oh I am so lonely in this mind.

*(Blackout with loud rumbling.*

*Lights up on Cordelia in the stage-right chair and Regan on the stage-left bench with Goneril on her knees before them, panting and in distress.*

*Faint organ music ["In Nomine a 5, No. 3" by William Byrd] plays over soft rumbling.)*

Where have you been?

GONERIL: In the storm.

REGAN: Did you find Dad?

GONERIL: No.

REGAN: Then why did you come back?

GONERIL: I couldn't remember how to live.

REGAN: You're lucky we don't execute you.

GONERIL: I would slaughter you all.

I did find something.

CORDELIA: What did you find?

GONERIL: A thing.

REGAN: What kind of thing.

*(The music fades out slowly.)*

GONERIL *(Getting up and going to Regan)*: Nothing can protect you from nothing. When everything falls away, there is . . . there is . . . what is there. For so long, something was protecting me, and that something turned out to be God which turned out to be a curse, which is what I have. I am cursed with nothing and would give up my life for some distraction but there is no distraction left. I tried to embrace the nothingness but there was nothing to embrace, only pride in the act of embracing, and pride is the greatest nothing of all. How I longed to seek and find goodness and how much goodness I found but it was nothing as well. She held my hand and I held nothing.

*(Goneril caresses Regan's face.)*

She wept tears of compassion on my poor old brow and they turned to nothing even as I wiped her sweet eyes and loved her as only a father can love.

*(Regan pushes Goneril's hand away.*
*Goneril turns away and starts walking to the throne, panting oddly.)*

REGAN: Help. I will pray and it will work once, and then I will pray again and it will not work a second time. This is how prayer works.

*(Goneril sits on the throne. This should be the first time in the show that anyone sits there.)*

GONERIL: I am Lear!

*(Regan runs out. Faint harpsichord music ["Pavana Lachrimae" by John Dowland, set by William Byrd] begins.)*

Cordelia, I don't like it!
CORDELIA: What?
GONERIL: This picking up lovers, moving in with them, dumping them. What is that?
CORDELIA: What about Regan? She's the biggest slut!
GONERIL: What was wrong with France?

*(Pause.*
   *Goneril hits Cordelia's shoulder.)*

CORDELIA: I don't know!

GONERIL: What do you mean you don't know? You must know.

CORDELIA: I was in love with him, and then suddenly one day he just grossed me out.

GONERIL: You can't break up just because of that.

CORDELIA: Desperately wanting someone out of your life isn't a good reason to break up?

GONERIL: How do you think I liked being married to a nut-job like your mother for fifty years? You think that was a piece of cake?

CORDELIA: Why didn't you leave her?

GONERIL: Because she was my wife and my responsibility and a man doesn't leave his wife and children on the street.

CORDELIA: How could you choose to live in misery?

GONERIL: It's not so bad. You kids think romance is everything. Romance is nothing!

CORDELIA: Today people actually value personal happiness.

GONERIL: Let's see how happy you are when you're dying alone.

CORDELIA: Who says I'm dying alone?

GONERIL: You could have made it work with France!

CORDELIA: France was cheating on me.

GONERIL: What man doesn't cheat on his wife? What the hell's the matter with you? How can you be so naive?

CORDELIA: What's your point?

GONERIL: When you get to be my age you realize that having children is the only thing that matters. If you wait too long you'll have miscarriages. You don't want that kind of freakish life!

*(Pause. The lights go red. There is a loud, scary bass throbbing noise.)*

Fuck you! I hope your womb turns into testicles!

*(Back to normal light, soft rumbling.)*

CORDELIA: Help! Someone help!

*(Edgar and Edmund run in.*
*Faint consort music ["The King of Denmark, his Galliard" by John Dowland] begins.)*

GONERIL: Here are France and Burgundy!
Hey guys, there's no more money!
EDMUND AND EDGAR: What?
GONERIL: You don't get money to marry that stupid banished cunt!

*(Regan wanders in slowly, smiling crazily.)*

And she has crabs and gonorrhea which she got from fucking all the horses!
CORDELIA: I did not!
GONERIL: She made all the horses fuck her in the ass and then she sucked her poop off their dicks!
CORDELIA: I didn't! She's making that up!
EDMUND: I don't want her if she comes without any money!

*(Edmund exits.)*

EDGAR: Well I have plenty of money already, so I'll take her. Come with me, Cordelia.

*(Edgar tugs on Cordelia's arm. She doesn't budge.)*

I'm a dolphin.
CORDELIA: What?

*(The music cuts out.)*

EDGAR: I'm a dolphin! Do you want to give me a fish? Here is my dolphin language.

*(Edgar makes dolphin noises.)*

GONERIL: You're not a dolphin!

*(Edgar makes dolphin noises.)*

EDGAR: I'm saying, "Hi Goneril! Nice to meet you!"

GONERIL *(Towering over Edgar, screaming)*: I AM LEAR!!!

*(Edgar cringes away, then abruptly turns on Cordelia.)*

EDGAR: Are you going to touch my orangutang?

CORDELIA: What?

EDGAR: My orangutang. Because you can't touch my orangutang because it's mine and you can't touch it and only the king can touch it or I'll chop off your legs!

CORDELIA: Don't worry, I won't touch it!

EDGAR: You better not!

*(Edgar makes dolphin noises.)*

That's me warning you!

*(Edgar goes to the dais. Throughout the following exchange between the sisters, he removes his ruff, cape, neck chain, and sword and dumps them by the side of the dais.)*

GONERIL *(Leaving the throne and coming downstage)*: Nothing can protect you from nothing!

*(Regan runs to the throne and sits down.)*

You must replace and replace and replace and replace I replace your face Goneril! Regan I replace you! There will be something about daughters turning their backs on their fathers and they will not listen to me. Goneril, listen! Regan, listen!

*(Regan leaves the throne and joins Goneril and Cordelia.)*

I humbly apologize for daring to ask for a fraction of what used to be wholly mine before I gave it to you all!

CORDELIA: I hope you two had fun torturing our father! He had no idea what cunts the two of you really are!

GONERIL: Oh go fuck yourself, Cordelia!

*(Goneril returns to the throne and sits.)*

REGAN: Yeah whatever fuckface. Why don't you go fuck a parrot?

CORDELIA: You fuck a parrot, Parrot-Fucker!

REGAN *(Screaming in an unbelievably terrifying manner)*: YOU FUCK A PARROT!!!

CORDELIA *(Tearfully)*: You fuck a parrot!

EDGAR: And when I look into a monkey's eyes, I can see the future. I can see dinosaurs and Fourth of July fireworks. And I realize that we are all dependent upon each other in one gigantic ecosystem of natural intelligence.

These are just a few of the humble thoughts I have. God bless the earth.

GONERIL *(To Edgar)*: I taught them to love trees, and the love they feel for trees feeds their evil hearts.

EDGAR: They are not really happy. What they have is not true happiness.

GONERIL: Yes, yes it is.

*(Edmund enters with his sword held up.)*

EDMUND: If you come beside me, I will stand up for you and hold up my sword of righteousness. You need only to come with me and you will find something far greater than all your parts. You will find a knock-kneed badger! With antlers on!

*(The lights go red. A high-pitched tone plays.*

*Goneril stands up from the throne and motions for Edmund to approach the dais. He hands her his sword, which she holds above her head as if she's about to knight him.*

*Regan gently pushes his head downwards, as if guiding him to bow, and then shoves his head roughly down onto the dais at Goneril's feet. Edmund's upper body is hidden beneath Goneril's skirt. Goneril stomps on him hard and he screams in pain.*

*All sound cuts out.*

*Lights out except for lit candles and a spotlight on Cordelia sitting on the stage-right bench.)*

CORDELIA: Green grass grows on the bottom of my yard and I believe that there was a bowl of roses on the table filled with violet-water, and these were the types of details that people paid attention to because there was the time and space for it. Everyone had children and a family and a loaf of bread in the oven and fights and the cock-blocking of the grandfather as he attempted to charm the nurses and perhaps that was the, perhaps that was a way to show love but I don't know, sometimes I think the way to show love is to be loving. You just paint and paint and paint your face until your face goes away, and that makes me think about a few things, such as wondering whether we will ever become the kind of adults who drive a bus and go to school for community issues and trying to make things more cultural for the benefit of all humankind. I don't know. There are so many issues to ponder when I have a feeling that I am avoiding something I must not avoid but of course I will avoid it, because I am above all things a coward and a cunt who fights and fights her fates during the temporary blinding that occurred when the lowlifes got hold of her head and pushed. If someone pushes my head into a ditch full of ditchwater, then so what?

*(Back to red light. Goneril stomps on Edmund again. Soft rumbling.)*

GONERIL: I was happy once, and my being wept with gratitude for I was forsaken and lost, and somehow I managed to smile my ghoulish smile without all my teeth falling out, which is a blessing. One day my teeth will be harvested like corn from its husk, and I shall remember the sweetness of being able to smile with teeth and show my humanity, the loathsomeness of my existence.

*(Stage lights and house lights suddenly bump on, as if the show is over. All sound cuts out.*

*Edmund, Regan and Goneril hold their positions from the end of the last scene.*

*From this point forward, until they turn into characters from Sesame Street, the actors "play themselves" and are referred to in the script by the names of the actors in the show's original cast.)*

PAUL *(The actor who played Edgar, to the audience)*: We enjoy watching horrible things. It gives us a feeling of immunity.

*(Edmund, Regan and Goneril exit.*
*Paul removes his false mustache and beard. He walks into the audience.)*

You're all so young. Even if you think you're old, you're not. Please enjoy this time, I beg you. Please enjoy this time.

You don't know where your path will lead or which is the right one. If you make a mistake, then you will arrive at the same place of unknowing in a few years, and if you make another mistake then the same thing will happen again. And each year that passes in fruitlessness, you will decrease in value. And what if you never find the right path? It happens. Almost nobody's dreams actually come true. You have to learn acceptance. But that doesn't always come, you know?

What are you doing with your life? Every minute, every second of the day. This is your one chance. What are you doing? What are you doing here? Is this really what you want to be doing with your life? Being here? Doing this? If not . . . then go. Run. Run away and do something better.

*(The following lines should be made to sound like an ad-lib:)*

I'm totally serious. Don't feel like you have to be polite. If there's something else you'd rather be doing with your life, then please, go with our blessing. I'm gonna step backstage for a minute or two and then I'll be back. *(Name of light operator)*, would you please bring down the stage lights?

*(Paul exits and remains offstage for at least a full minute.*
*He reenters and walks into the audience.)*

Any moment, any moment now it will come. The thing will happen that is the thing that crushes. It could be happening now. We could be . . . we could be sitting here and the worst could be occurring.

We shut out people's pain when we are not in pain ourselves. We wear an armor that is false, that is constructed of nothing and when the lies shatter we will face it. And we will survive by continuing on, by forgetting, by shutting out, but we will not forget. We will not have not forgotten anything. Everything that happened will be contained somewhere inside us, feeding on us, waiting for the day in which it can regain its rightful power.

*(Big Bird, formerly Edmund, enters bent over upside down and walking backward. He holds onto his ankles with his hands and talks through his legs to Gordon, formerly Edgar/Paul.)*

BIG BIRD: Oh, hi Gordon!

*(Gordon walks back onstage. The house lights fade out.)*

GORDON: Oh, hi Big Bird! Uh . . .
BIG BIRD: Nice day, isn't it?
GORDON: Yeah, very nice! Big Bird?
BIG BIRD: Hm?
GORDON: Why are you doing that?
BIG BIRD: What?
GORDON: That!
BIG BIRD: Oh!
GORDON: With your head between your legs!
BIG BIRD: Oh. Because.
GORDON: Because why?
BIG BIRD: Just because.
GORDON: You're standing with your head between your legs just because? Uh, can't you give me a better reason than "just because"?
BIG BIRD: Well, I guess I could try, but I don't think I could come up with a better reason.
GORDON: Yeah, I understand.
BIG BIRD: You know what I'm gonna do now?
GORDON: What?
BIG BIRD: This!

*(Big Bird makes the following noise with an accompanying silly gesture that takes him offstage.)*

Dee-do! Dee-do! Dee-do! Dee-do! Dee-do! Dee-do!

*(Gordon watches Big Bird exit, shrugs, and imitates the noise and gesture, which takes him offstage.)*

GORDON: Dee-do! Dee-do! Dee-do! Dee-do! Dee-do! Dee-do!

*(Okwui, formerly Goneril; April, formerly Regan; and Amelia, formerly Cordelia, enter without their wigs.)*

OKWUI: The best part of *King Lear* is when Lear's daughter Cordelia dies, and Lear comes in and goes like this:

Howl, howl, howl, howl! O, you are men of stones!
Had I your tongues and eyes, I'd use them so
That Heaven's vault should crack. She's gone forever!
I know when one is dead, and when one lives;
She's dead as earth. Lend me a looking glass;
If that her breath will mist or stain the stone,
Why, then she lives.

This feather stirs; she lives! If it be so,
It is a chance which does redeem all sorrows
That ever I have felt.

A plague upon you, murderers, traitors all!
I might have saved her; now she's gone forever!
Cordelia, Cordelia! stay a little. Ha?
What is't thou sayst? Her voice was ever soft,
Gentle, and low, an excellent thing in woman.
I killed the slave that was a-hanging thee.

And my poor fool is hanged! No, no, no life?
Why should a dog, a horse, a rat, have life,
And thou no breath at all? Thou'lt come no more,
Never, never, never, never, never!

Pray you, undo this button. Thank you, sir.
Do you see this? Look on her, look, her lips,
Look there, look there!

*(To April and Amelia)* And then he dies.

AMELIA: Wow.
APRIL: That made me really sad.
OKWUI: Yeah. And it feels kinda good, too, you know?

*(Gordon enters. As he speaks, Maria, formerly Goneril/Okwui; and Olivia, formerly Cordelia/Amelia, pull out the side benches and place them in an upside-down V-shape facing downstage.)*

GORDON: Look, look, I'm telling you she's a great candidate! She says that she's against big spending, big business, and inflation. She says when she gets in the office, there will be enough money for government, social programs, and a space program!
SUSAN *(Formerly Regan/April)*: That sounds great, what's her name?
MARIA: Alice in Wonderland!

*(They all laugh. Big Bird enters holding papers. Gordon, Susan, Maria and Olivia sit on the benches facing the audience. Big Bird stands in the middle between them.)*

BIG BIRD: Hey, it's time for your presents!

*(Everyone reacts: "Presents?" etc.)*

Yeah . . . well, I just uh, drew pictures of all my grown-up friends on Sesame Street. And I'm going to give them to you.

*(Everyone reacts: "Aww, that's great," etc.)*

I'm going to be an artist when I grow up.

*(Everyone reacts: "Great. Great," etc.)*

SUSAN: You're good too.

*(Big Bird hands Susan her picture.)*

Oh—that's gotta be me.

*(Susan shows everyone her picture.)*

GORDON: There's Susan.
BIG BIRD: Yeah, that's—you're always smiling, Susan.
MARIA: That's good. That's good.

*(Big Bird hands Olivia her picture.)*

OLIVIA: Oh hey, there I am. Hey, that's nice!

*(Olivia shows everyone her picture.)*

BIG BIRD: You like it, Olivia? I made y—I put musical notes, 'cause you're singing.
OLIVIA: I see. Thank you, Big Bird.

*(Big Bird hands Maria her picture.)*

Oh, I know who that is . . .
MARIA: Is that me? Oh, well, yes . . .

*(Maria shows everyone her picture.)*

GORDON: Oh, that's beautiful.
MARIA: Thank you, Big Bird, thank you.

*(Big Bird hands Gordon his picture.)*

GORDON: Hey, wait, whoa . . .

*(Gordon shows everyone his picture.)*

BIG BIRD: That's you, Gordon.
OLIVIA: A little young, don't you think?

*(Gordon laughs.)*

BIG BIRD: And, last but not least, ta-da!

*(Big Bird holds up a picture of an elderly bald man with glasses.)*

MARIA: Oh look at that one, that's nice.
OLIVIA: Big Bird, that's so beautiful.
SUSAN: That's great!
GORDON: That is really nice. Can I see it Big Bird?

*(Gordon looks closely at the drawing.)*

That's terrific, it really looks like him.
SUSAN: It sure does.
OLIVIA: Yeah, you captured him.
MARIA: Wow, that's, that's beautiful, Big Bird. Really nice.
BIG BIRD: Well thank you. Thank you.
GORDON: Wonderful.
BIG BIRD: Well, I can't wait till he sees it.

*(Awkward pause.)*

Say, where is he? I wanna give it to him. I know! He's in the
store.
GORDON: Uh, Big Bird? He's, he's not in there.
BIG BIRD: Oh. Then where is he?
MARIA: Big Bird . . . uh, don't you remember we told you? Uh, Mr.
Hooper died. He, he's dead.
BIG BIRD: Oh yeah, I remember. Well, I'll give it to him when he
comes back.
SUSAN: Big Bird, Mr Hooper's not coming back.
BIG BIRD: Why not?

*(Susan goes to Big Bird and puts her arm around him.)*

SUSAN: Big Bird, when people die . . . they don't come back.
BIG BIRD: Ever?

SUSAN: No, never.

BIG BIRD: Well, why not?

OLIVIA *(Fighting tears)*: Well, Big Bird . . . they're dead. They, they can't come back.

BIG BIRD: Well, he's got to come back! Why, who's gonna take care of the store? And who's gonna make my birdseed milkshakes and tell me stories?

OLIVIA: Big Bird, I'm gonna take care of the store. Mr. Hooper, he left it to me. And I'll make you your milkshakes and we'll all tell you stories, and we'll make sure you're okay.

SUSAN: Sure, we'll look after you.

BIG BIRD: Oh. Hm.

Well . . . it won't be the same.

*(Gordon goes to Big Bird.)*

GORDON *(Fighting tears)*: You're right, Big Bird. It's, it's, it'll never be the same around here without him. But you know something? We can all be very happy that we had a chance to be with him . . . and to know him . . .

BIG BIRD: Yeah.

GORDON: . . . and to love him a lot, when he was here.

BIG BIRD: Yeah.

OLIVIA: And Big Bird, we still have our memories of him.

BIG BIRD: Well, yeah. Yeah, our memories. Right. Why, memories, that's how I drew this picture—from memory.

OLIVIA: It's good, yeah.

*(Everyone makes noises of agreement.)*

BIG BIRD: Yeah. And, and we can remember him and remember him and remember him . . . as much as we want to!

*(He looks at the picture.)*

But I don't like it. It makes me sad.

MARIA: We all feel sad, Big Bird.

BIG BIRD: Hmm. He's . . . never coming back?

SUSAN: Never.

BIG BIRD: Well, I don't understand! You know, everything was just fine! Why does it have to be this way? Give me one good reason!

GORDON: Big Bird . . . it has to be this way . . . because.

BIG BIRD: Just . . . because?

GORDON: Just, because.

BIG BIRD *(Looking at the picture)*: You know, I'm gonna miss you, Mr. Looper.

MARIA *(Smiling, in tears)*: That's "Hooper," Big Bird, "Hooper."

*(Everyone laughs softly.)*

BIG BIRD: You're right.

*(Everyone gathers around Big Bird, and they all share a big, silent hug.*
*Everyone leaves the stage except Pete, formerly Edmund/Big Bird.*
*Pete crosses downstage. As he speaks to the audience, the lights slowly fade until there is only a small, intense pool around him.)*

PETE: He is alive I must remember that he is alive. He is alive and I must remember, I must get to the thing that is the thing, and that thing is when he is gone there will be no more, nothing. Nobody loves you like your father does, there is no other father other than the one you have who was your dad all your life who loved you that is your dad. There is no other one. And my father is dying and I don't know, I don't know I must remember that he is . . . he is still alive. I can still hear his voice. I can pick up the telephone any time I want and hear his voice and some day pretty soon I will not be able to do that. I must remember that he is still alive and I can pick up the phone and we can talk but there is nothing to talk about. I ask about his health and he tells me and sometimes it is bad news and sometimes good and then we don't know what to talk about anymore. Five minutes. Every night it is five to seven minutes of my parents' voices on the phone, and that's it. I think my mother would like to talk for longer but my dad always says, "Okay," and cuts it off so that it won't be a burden to me, which it is. I am one of the fortunate ones because my mother prays for me, she prays for me incessantly with her friends and I feel blessed, I felt blessed I no longer do. God was a figment of my egotism. And now I am . . . I can't stand to see him smile. I can't stand to see him struggle over fixing the stove to save money. And I helped him put this . . . there was this . . . it's an electric stove where you have to stick this faceplate on, and once you stick it on it's permanent. So my father and I very nervously stuck it on and then it didn't work. And the whole time I was praying (this was back when I still believed in God), "Please Lord, let him fix it. Please let him fix it. Let it work." And it worked, and he was so happy. It's such a terrible thing to see him happy. He. . . I just prayed. And it worked. But it didn't work because there is no God there is no longer any God. I should send him a book or something. I don't know why I don't do more for him. I will regret it so much when he is gone. I will miss him so much, and all of this wasted time, all of this wasted time in which I didn't want to talk to him, I didn't want to spend time with him, I didn't even want to eat meals with him. And I . . . we would fight because he would . . . I would . . . they would be eating breakfast and I would just grab some cereal and go back downstairs, sometimes without even saying good morning. What manners. How did I become so rude, so selfish, so . . . when did I become this person who doesn't say good morning? And the same thing with lunch, they would be eating and just . . . I don't know how to love people, I never have. If I keep going down this road, nothing will ever truly make me happy. I must remember that I will never hear my father's voice again or see his face or be able to ask him any questions. I should go into the room where he's watching television and talk to him but . . . it is so hard to go in there, it is so hard to be around him, I can't even hug him, I can't look at him. He is such a gifted man, a special man, and nobody . . . he has nobody to listen to him talk. And I will end up that way if I'm not careful, if I don't change, if I allow this egotism to consume me. Everything that happens to his body will happen to mine. It's happening already. I look older. I've gotten used to lying half awake, in and out of nightmares, waking up unharmed but not safe. You create your . . . you think you are creating reality through the words you use and the storics you tell but you are not creating realities, you have no idea what the fuck is going on, there are certain facts, certain facts you can hang on to but nothing else really. I can't imagine what it will be like when he is dying. I will have to be there all the time. I will have to be perfect. I . . . when he is gone that loss is going to be too much. You can't lose that much. When he was in the eighth grade he got recruited into a high school marching band to play the piccolo and was asked to perform in a show that same week. Usually the older students taught the younger ones how to play their instruments but nobody knew how to play the piccolo so nobody taught him, and yet he was supposed to perform. So he just marched, the smallest person in the band with the smallest instrument, and pretended to play the piccolo. For a year. He would pick it up and pretend to play whenever the flutist picked up his flute. And he tried to teach himself at home how to play but it was really hard and he could never try playing aloud with the band because the piccolo makes a "shrilling sound" that can be heard from miles away. And he never went to band practice because what was the point, and nobody ever said anything to him about it. He stayed on for a year because the band always got taken out for noodles after performances. But he finally quit after his friends made fun of him. They were like, "What is that tiny thing you're playing?"

*(Blackout.*

*Echoey, distorted cover of Gram Parsons' "Big Mouth Blues" [performed by Tim Simmonds] begins to play.*

*The following strobe light/blackout sequence should convey the sense of clips from old-home movies cutting in and out.*

*Strobe light on Pete laughing downstage left.*

*Blackout.*

*Strobe light on Pete on the floor, leaning against the stage-left bench and daydreaming.*

*Blackout.*

*Strobe light on Pete walking downstage and smiling to himself.*

*Blackout.*

*Strobe light on Pete on the floor ducking behind the stage-right bench excitedly as if in the middle of a snowball fight.*

*Blackout.*

*Strobe light on Pete standing and stretching contentedly down-stage right.*

*Blackout.*

*Strobe light on Pete standing upstage left encouraging an imaginary toddler walking toward him.*

*Blackout.*

*Strobe light on Pete upstage center watching eagerly for a loved one's arrival. He catches sight of the person and waves excitedly.*

*Blackout.*

*Lights up on Pete in the middle of the stage. The other actors sit on the benches, which Pete moved during last blackout to be parallel with the front of the stage. They sit facing Pete with their backs to us, as if they are an extension of the audience.)*

I'll miss you. I'll miss you. I'll miss you. I'll miss you. I'll miss you. I'll miss you. I'll miss you. I'll miss you. I'll miss you. I'll miss you.

*(Blackout.)*

END OF PLAY

Young Jean Lee has directed her plays throughout the U.S. and Europe for Young Jean Lee's Theater Company (www.youngjeanlee.org). She is a member of New Dramatists and 13P, and has an MFA from Mac Wellman's playwriting program at Brooklyn College. She is the recipient of the Zuercher Theater Spektakel's ZKB Patronage Prize, the OBIE's Emerging Playwright Award, and the American Academy of Arts and Letters Academy Award.